GET THAT
NIGGER
OFF THE FIELD

GET THAT NIGGER OFF THE FIELD

An Oral History of Black Ballplayers
from the Negro Leagues to the
Present

by

ART RUST, JR.

Book Mail Services

Book Mail Services
1000 Dean Street
Brooklyn, NY 11238

Shadow Lawn Press
8469 Hollywood Boulevard
Los Angeles, California 90069

Library-of-Congress Cataloging-in-Publication Data

Rust, Art, 1927—
    "Get that nigger off the field!"

    Includes index.
    1. Baseball—Biography. 2. Negro athletes—Biography. I. Title.
GV865.A1R87   1992   796.357'092'2   [B]   75-38513

ISBN 0-912-33119-4

Printed in the United States of America

1 2 3 4 5 6 7 8 9 A B C D E F G

distributed by
Golden-Lee Books

produced by
Shadow Lawn Press

This book is dedicated to the loving memories of my wife Edna, my mother Una, and my father Arthur, Senior . . . all of whom lived my dream with me and made possible this tribute to America's unsung heroes.

Contents

Author's Note

"Get that nigger off the field!" Chicago White Stockings manager Adrian "Cap" Anson bellowed at black baseball star Fleetwood Walker of the Toledo Blue Stockings in an exhibition game over a hundred years ago. Anson's refusal to play against teams that fielded black players led to the unwritten "gentlemen's agreement" that kept blacks out of professional baseball until 1946. In a previous testament to the mean-spiritedness of Cap Anson's attitudes, I called the first edition of this book *Get That Nigger Off the Field* when it was first published in 1976. It raised a lot of hackles then and caused a lot of comment. People were enraged that I dared use the word "nigger" in my book title.

Things haven't changed much in fifteen years as this revised and expanded second edition of my book goes to press. Bill White may sit in the president's chair at the National League offices, Hank Aaron may sit in the vice-president's chair over at the Atlanta Braves' office, Douglas Wilder may sit in the governor's chair in the capitol of the old Confederate South, but I have a harder time using the word "nigger" in my own book today than I did in 1976.

People are afraid of the word "nigger." In these times of political correctness when words do indeed have the power to kill, "nigger" carries an especial malevolence. But "nigger" is what the white man called us and niggers are what we were in his eyes. He has to live with the weight of nigger today, just as we lived with it and continue to do so. The word "nigger" unites both the racist and victim of racism in a single bond.

The bookstore owners tell me that I dare not use the word "nigger" because I might offend the black customers who would otherwise buy this book. Hell, black people know what a nigger is because they're called it silently every day of their lives. We live with it in the same way every other racial group lives with the epithets that have been used by their oppressors to define them. I say, rather, that most people are afraid that I'll offend the white customers who don't want to be caught leafing through a book that has "nigger" on the cover. Too much shame; too much guilt.

So this time around, in the spirit of political correctness, they said, "Don't be offensive." But I decided that I'd rather be honest than inoffensive. So *Get That Nigger Off the Field* is what it remains.

Art Rust, Jr.
New York, 1991

INTRODUCTION TO THE FIRST EDITION

The reader will find it interesting to look at baseball and life through the eyes of a black youngster growing up with major league baseball in New York and learning that the game, like life in this country, is not the total example of sportsmanship and competitiveness it claims to be. Art Rust, Jr. takes us through the 1880s, when whites and blacks competed on the field until a Hall-of-Famer, Cap Anson, decided to institute a "no-play" edict against blacks. That lasted until Jackie Robinson was signed by a progressive-thinking Branch Rickey in 1946. My own personal professional baseball experiences started six years later . . . facing open hostility in Virginia, Oklahoma, Texas, North Carolina, and Louisiana . . . and the sometimes subtle prejudices of Arizona, Kansas, Colorado, and even California.

In his interviews with various black stars, Art points out the meager bonuses paid to blacks, the tough job of having to adjust to being sent to hostile communities to play, the lack of black benchwarmers, and the lack of opportunities in baseball for blacks once their careers are finished. (This is still a fact, despite Frank Robinson's being named manager of the Cleveland Indians at the end of the 1974 season.) Most of all, though, the reader will get a look at some baseball history—both black and white—and read personal interviews with some great and near great black players. *Get That Nigger Off the Field* is the first book I've read that looks at baseball from a black man's point of view.

Bill White
New York, 1976

FOREWORD

My friend and present writing colleague, Art Rust, Jr., has revised his book on famous black ballplayers and their stories. Art has covered almost forty-five years of major league baseball history in which some of my heroes say things about the sport that certainly surprised me with their frankness but at the same time didn't surprise me at all. They are recounting the same things about baseball that a lot of players may have felt but never talked about in public. From reading these stories, it seems as if what Cleon Jones and Larry Doby described about their own pasts I can attest to from my experiences. And I was fascinated to learn that early in their respective careers Cleon Jones, Larry Doby, and even Don Newcombe bore the same sort of criticisms that Henry Aaron, Dave Winfield, and Dave Parker were subjected to years later. From reading their stories, I know I'm in some very good company.

Young people may not realize that it has been a long, long road for African-American athletes in major league sports. And the road is longer still. We've had to overcome a lot of hostility just to win the opportunity to play on the same fields or in the same buildings with white athletes. And we're facing some of the same discrimination now when it comes to getting jobs in management, in the team organizations, and in the league offices themselves. There is plenty of room for everybody in the front offices and coaching systems of baseball franchises, and I look forward to the day when black athletes can expect the same opportunities that await white athletes at the end of their playing careers. I hope readers of all backgrounds find these stories as enlightening as I did.

Darryl Strawberry
Los Angeles, 1991

PREFACE

Every time I walk down St. Nicholas Avenue between 145th and 141st Streets, where I lived, the memories keep jumping out at me. The stickball games, the black Joe DiMaggios, the black Mel Otts, the black Harry Dannings; the great Mel Allen and Red Barber broadcasts of the Yankee and Dodger games; running up to the newsstand every Friday afternoon to get the Sporting News, *which at that time was an all-baseball publication. It was the ambition and desire of all of us to play major league baseball. I'm certain some of us could have made it. If that stretch of St. Nicholas Avenue (then called Sugar Hill) could talk, it would sum it all up for me and the rest of the black kids on the block.*

My first recollection of major league baseball is of 1933, when as a six-year-old I listened to the World Series between the New York Giants vs. the Washington Senators on the radio. My father, Arthur Senior, was a St. Louis Cardinals fanatic. This came about in 1924, when he was fresh off the boat from his native Montego Bay, Jamaica. His brother-in-law took him to his first baseball game at the Polo Grounds, where the Giants were meeting the Cardinals. Thus began the love affair.

It was opening day at home for the New York Giants as they took on the Boston Braves. On this particular occasion, April, 1935, my father and I were sitting in the right-field grandstands at the Polo Grounds. It was snowing! I had on tan leather leggings, a Navy blue pea jacket, and an Eton cap. It was Babe Ruth's last active season in the major leagues. He was with the Boston Braves. Before that Ruth had twenty-one brilliant seasons with the Boston Red Sox and the New York Yankees. During the flag-raising ceremonies, my father made a special point to say to me, "There he is: Babe Ruth, the 'Bambino,' the 'Sultan of Swat.'" My father also pointed out some of the other Braves: Shanty Hogan, Danny MacFayden, Wally Berger, and Rabbit Maranville. Then he showed me Mel Ott, Dick Bartell, Travis Jackson, Carl Hubbell, and Bill Terry on the Giants. Baseball, how I loved it!

Lodged in the pit of my mind were the Negro league games I attended as a child, and all those great figures: Josh Gibson, Satchel Paige, Judy Johnson, Buck Leonard, et. al. The games were played at the Polo Grounds, Yankee Stadium, and Randall's Island.

Brainwashing is a strange thing. I remember my general impression when I attended the National Negro League games at Yankee Stadium and the Polo Grounds. It was more like a carnival: blacks eating chicken, drinking heavily, women overdressed, everybody raunchy as hell. Typical Negro league behavior? No, not really. I saw whites behaving the same way at their ball games. Boy, did whitey have my head!

As a black youngster I would say to myself, "Josh Gibson was just as good—if not superior to—Yankee Bill Dickey . . . Satch Paige is just as good as the Yankee Red Ruffing . . . then why can't they play in the big leagues?"

Nineteen forty. All the guys from St. Nicholas Avenue are playing baseball in the lot next door to the Polo Grounds, home of our boyhood idols: Mel Ott, Carl Hubbell, Dick Bartell, and scads of others. Here's a ballpark in Harlem and not one black man can play major league ball in there. I can't figure it out.

July, 1941. My mother is ironing in the kitchen. I'm in my room listening to the All-Star Game from Briggs Stadium in Detroit. I'm happy right now. I'm a National League fan and they're ahead. Arky Vaughan has just hit his second home run for the National Leaguers. Then all of a sudden in the bottom of the ninth, up steps Red Soxer Ted Williams who smashes one over the top of the roof in right field off Cub right-hander Claude Passeau. I remember sitting there in tears and my mother laughing at me and saying, "What the hell are you getting so upset over the white man's game for anyway?"

On St. Nicholas Avenue in Manhattan between 145th and 141st Streets, everybody fashioned himself after some white ballplayer. I was Marty "Slats" Marion, Cardinal shortstop. My cousin Irving was Yankee second baseman Joe Gordon; Sonny Curtis was Yankee pitcher Red Ruffing; Junior Manning was Giant catcher Harry "the Horse" Danning. But what the hell were we talking about? Blacks didn't play in the major leagues; we were all deluding ourselves.

April, 1942. Looking out the window of 654 St. Nicholas Avenue. There is a Railway Express truck with my spike shoes from the Ridell Sporting Goods Store in St. Louis. Saved up my allowance ... all of $15. God damn, what a thrill! My own baseball shoes! Now I can go to St. Nicholas Park and make like Marty Marion.

Baseball. The game was my life. At one time I wanted to be a major league ballplayer, but I was black and playing in the

Negro National League just did not appeal to me. As a young black idolizing white ballplayers, I readily recall many indignities that were suffered in the Polo Grounds and Yankee Stadium. At Yankee Stadium in 1939, while leaning over the bleacher wall in right field with other youngsters seeking autographs, Washington Senator outfielder Taft Wright called me a "black son of a bitch" when I put my scorecard in front of his face. At the Polo Grounds I was called a "black bastard" by St. Louis Cardinal left-hander Clyde Shoun when I was trying to get his autograph. My head was rubbed for good luck by St. Louis Cardinal right-hander Fiddler Bill McGee as he walked out of the clubhouse past the bleachers. These humiliations really shook up this eleven-year-old.

In September, 1941, while attending Edward W. Stitt Junior High School in Washington Heights, one of my science teachers, Arthur Triffon, used to allow me to leave school early to go to the ball games at the Polo Grounds, which at that time started at three o'clock. I'll never forget his saying to me one day, "How could you get so involved in a sport that doesn't let Negroes play?" I really had no answer. How can one describe his reasons for being in love? I recall that on this particular occasion, the Cardinals were in town, and being a Cardinal fan was something that Mr. Triffon could not really fathom. "You root for a team of crackers—you've got to be nuts," he said.

I remember a Negro National League game at Yankee Stadium in July, 1937, where I saw the Pittsburgh Crawfords' hard-hitting Josh Gibson hit a homer off of the Philadelphia Stars' beanpole left-hander Stuart "Slim" Jones. The ball went over the left-field bullpen and out of the stadium. I was amazed. I said to myself, "He should be in the major leagues." I have always been convinced that Jackie Robinson was not the first black in the modern major leagues. The Washington Senators in the mid-thirties and early forties were loaded with Latin American players of darker hue who, because they spoke Spanish, "got away with it" in the big time.

I'm sitting behind home plate at the Polo Grounds. Giants are playing the Cardinals. Cuban Mike Gonzales is in the third-base coaches' box for St. Louis. Hey, what the hell's he doing out there? He's a light-skinned black man. My father is the same color. Oh, I forgot—Gonzales speaks Spanish . . . so that means he isn't a black man.

The Senators were the first major league franchise to scout and exploit the Caribbean area and the Latin American countries for baseball talent. Joe Cambria, their chief scout, did a thorough job of it by finding players like Roberto Estalella and Roberto Ortiz and other chocolate-colored Cubans, and Alex Carrasquel from Caracas, Venezuela. All were black so far as I was concerned, but hell, they were not "niggers"—they spoke Spanish. That was the white rationale for allowing them to play. Let's say that Jackie Robinson was the first *American* black in the modern big leagues. I recall Estalella having a hard time of it every time the Senators visited the St. Louis Browns in Sportsman's Park. It was beanball after beanball. Did somebody know something? Let's see now. One of Estalella's teammates on the Senators, John Welaj, told me, "Everybody on the club knew that Roberto was black."

In 1939 I had one hell of a baseball scrapbook, filled to the brim with pictures of lily-white baseball players. I remember how proudly I carried it under my arm to the Polo Grounds. Walking jauntily up St. Nicholas Avenue past St. Nicholas Place, then to the ballpark. I recall I used to send away to George Burke, a photographer in Chicago who specialized in major league pictures. I had photos of every St. Louis Cardinal player from

1939 to 1942. I'll never forget Enos "Country" Slaughter signing a picture for me and walking down Eighth Avenue muttering, "How did that little nigger get all those pictures?" I said to myself, "With all those crackers, ain't no way a black guy's gonna play ball in the majors."

I remember Branch Rickey around 1939, then with the St. Louis Cardinals, putting his arm around me outside the parking lot next to the Polo Grounds and telling me that one day Negro ballplayers would appear in the majors. I looked up at him and smiled. I remember saying, "I don't think it will happen." I just thought it wouldn't be allowed in my lifetime.

Playing ball on St. Nicholas Avenue right across from number 654, where I lived. Junior Manning says he's Gabby Hartnett. My cousin Ernest Cobb is Mel Ott.; my other cousin Irving is Joe DiMaggio. Me, I'm Cardinal right-hander Lonnie Warneke. I have a big piece of bread stuck in my cheek, just like Warneke does with his tobacco. Black kids dreaming about the white man's game. Hell, all we had sportswise to think about was Joe Louis or Henry Armstrong, conquerors of the white world. If you ran swiftly, you'd say you were Jesse Owens. I do remember my attempt to break the Caucasian adulation barrier after a black Yankee game at the Stadium. There was a pitcher by the name of Schoolboy Taylor, a right-hander for the Philadelphia Stars who had a big kick like Van Lingle Mungo of the Brooklyn Dodgers. On St. Nicholas Avenue I was Schoolboy Taylor for the rest of the summer. I had broken an image barrier: I was now copying a black ballplayer.

There I was, a black kid on Sugar Hill in Harlem, eating, sleeping, and drinking baseball, and my people were not allowed to participate. I recall around 1939 when Washington Senator owner Clark Griffith gave this black kid a ray of hope when he talked with Josh Gibson and Buck Leonard in his office. Nothing came of it. Why didn't he just go ahead and hire them?

In the 1930s Wendell Smith, a black reporter for the *Pittsburgh Courier*, was carrying on his campaign to get "Negroes," as we called ourselves back then, in the majors. He personally told me he always thought that the Washington Senators might be the first to take a Negro. The city of Washington was about half black at that time. Wendell figured if half of the city boycotted the games at Griffith Stadium, the other half—all black—would attend.

In 1939 the Washington Senators' first baseman was Mickey Vernon and their first-string catcher was Rick Ferrell. Hell, Ferrell and Vernon couldn't carry Josh Gibson's and Buck Leonard's spike shoes. There was no written rule barring Negroes from organized baseball. What stopped him? I think there were two main reasons. One, about one-third of all major league players were Southerners and they would not play with or against blacks. (When Jackie Robinson was signed by the Dodgers, Leon "Red" Treadway, an outfielder belonging to the New York Giants who had a promising future in front of him, retired because of this.) Two, blacks could not travel with the big-league clubs because hotels in most cities would not accommodate them. Because of this, I thought the Negro leagues would be the only way for a black ballplayer to go.

June, 1937. Five days ago Joe Louis knocked out Jimmy Braddock in Chicago to become the heavyweight champion of the world. Joe and his wife, Marva, are walking up St. Nicholas Place. All the kids are running behind him. In the background lies the Polo Grounds, and it's a strange juxtaposition: Joe Louis, a black man, heavyweight champion of the world, and behind him a ballpark in the heart of the black community where no black man was allowed to play major league baseball—there or anywhere else.

Schedules in the Negro leagues were very irregular and games were vulnerable to sudden cancelation. Players were always jumping teams for richer offers in Mexico and other Latin leagues. Only the black equivalent of the All-Star Game, the East-West Game, was a sure success, drawing as many as 51,000 fans to Chicago's Comiskey Park in 1943. There was no secret why the black leagues started and why they endured. They started because white players threatened to quit rather than share the diamond with black men. In the late nineteenth century, Negro infielders wore shin guards because white opponents would try to spike them at every opportunity. Pitchers aimed at their heads and club owners finally sent them away rather than offend white ballplayers.

One day in 1936 I'm playing stickball on St. Nicholas Avenue when a guy we called "Bill the Cop," just off duty, speaks to my father and tells him that Giant manager Bill Terry has complained to the precinct commander that he doesn't want "nigger cops" patrolling the Polo Grounds either before, during, or after the games—and particularly not at the executive entrances. Even as a nine-year-old, I get the message.

St. Nicholas Avenue between 141st and 145th Streets still looks just about the same. The sewer tops that we used for bases are still there. We used to dodge between cars, playing stickball, but I doubt that the kids on the block can get through that maze of traffic now. Every nook, cranny, crevice, hydrant, sewer top, and edifice I associate with my growing-up period, my intense love of baseball, and ultimately my career. When I look up at the windows on the third floor of 654, where I lived . . . my God, the memories are overwhelming.

I never dreamed that a black kid could identify with a Jackie Robinson, Willie Mays, Hank Aaron, or Frank Robinson. My heroes were Marty "Slats" Marion, Terry Moore, Mel Ott, Carl

Hubbell—good men all. Now the black kids have a choice that I didn't have—a choice that is rightfully, sometimes painfully, theirs.

In the following pages I put down my experiences, dreams, pleasures, and agonies of growing up on Sugar Hill. In those days you were a doctor, lawyer, or civil servant: careers in which you could possibly succeed. The thought of being an actor was degrading. Who wants their child to portray a servant? A journalist—but only for a low-paying black paper. Athletics was only a game for children to play, and children must put aside games when they grow up.

I was a premed student in college—it didn't work for me. I tried law school—that didn't work for me either. In 1954 I auditioned for a sportscaster position at radio station WWRL in Woodside, Queens. When I was hired I felt as if I had "broken through" just as Jack Roosevelt Robinson from Cairo, Georgia, had done when Branch Rickey hired him.

I lived to see blacks elected to the Baseball Hall of Fame. I lived to see Emmett Ashford, the first black umpire. I lived to see Hank Aaron break Babe Ruth's home-run record and Maury Wills break Ty Cobb's stolen bases record. I lived to see Frank Robinson become the first black manager in the major leagues and then see Henry Aaron make it to the vice presidency of the Atlanta Braves. Although some of the interviews in this book were conducted before those happy events, the system *is* breaking—Henry Aaron even has a seat on Ted Turner's Board of Directors and Bill White has become the President of the National League.

I'm glad I've been here to see it, to tell of it, to record it. Many of the players I've interviewed for this book are no longer alive. In many cases, their words and the accounts of their times are among the final interviews they gave. This book, therefore, is a living record, an oral history, and the testaments to greatness of some of the finest players baseball has ever known. Now that some of the historic figures of the Negro leagues are dead, they can no longer speak for themselves. Their records speak for them, of course, as do their final words. The interviews in this book are some of those final words reproduced exactly as they said them.

However, an interesting development: My daughter Suzanne, who lived through many frustrations during my career as a sportswriter and sportscaster and who is now a producer, still wants to know—as she did when she was ten years old—why women can't participate in major league baseball . . .

FOR LOVE
OF THE GAME

"As the eighth commissioner of baseball, I say to you
with sorrow and regret, I apologize for the
injustice you were subjected to. Every
decent-thinking person in this country agrees.
Your contribution to baseball was the finest
kind because it was unselfish."

Fay Vincent, Negro League reunion,
Cooperstown, New York
New York Times, August 13, 1991

". . . these players—gathered at Cooperstown . . . for a
reunion and celebration of their careers and
their league—have chosen to call their coming
together "For Love of the Game."

New York Times, August 13, 1991

In 1859 the National Association of Baseball Players was
formed. This organization consisted of more than one hundred
baseball clubs in the North. The primary purpose of this group
was rule making for member clubs. Two-and-a-half years after
the Civil War, in December, 1867, the National Association of

Baseball Players held its annual convention in Philadelphia. It was a time when black men, a majority of them former slaves, had just had the right to vote bestowed upon them. Then and there the first color line in baseball was drawn, barring blacks and the clubs that they played for from membership. The Association survived only a few more years but its exclusion of blacks set the mold for its successor, the National Association of Professional Baseball Players. Formed in 1871, this new association never had a written rule against black players, but there existed a "gentlemen's agreement" barring blacks from this first professional league and from its successor, the National League.

Denied participation in the Association, the blacks organized their own league to play among themselves. By 1867 these teams were so well run, at least in the North, that in October of that year a "colored championship" series was held in Brooklyn. The Excelsiors of Philadelphia gained the championship by defeating the Brooklyn Uniques and the Brooklyn Monitors.

The first paid black player in professional baseball was John W. "Bud" Fowler. Born in Cooperstown, New York, in 1854, Fowler learned to play baseball around Hudson, New York. In 1872 Fowler played second base, left field, and caught for New Castle, Pennsylvania. For the next quarter of a century he barnstormed from east to west. Fowler was the first of more than thirty blacks who played in a white league before 1900, just before white men totally excluded the black player from their organized baseball structure. Like most of the gypsy-like ballplayers of his time, Fowler could play any position, but it was as a second baseman that he excelled. The white press then recognized him "as the equal of any of his contemporaries at that position."

In the 1880s quite a few blacks played ball with white clubs. The first were two brothers, Moses Fleetwood Walker and William Welday Walker. Both played with the Toledo Blue Stockings in the American Association, which in those days had major league recognition, so the brothers Walker were actually the first two blacks in major league baseball. On the other hand, sixty-five years later, Jack Roosevelt Robinson was the first black in *modern* major league baseball. Later on Fleetwood Walker played for Newark, which had on its club George Stovey, whom many consider to be the greatest black pitcher ever. In the 1880s there were about twenty black ballplayers active in organized baseball. Bud Fowler played for Keokuk and Binghamton. Charles Kelly, a first baseman, played for a club in Danville, Illinois. Buffalo had a second baseman named Frank Grant. In 1887, because of the feeling that more blacks would slowly but surely enter white organized baseball's structure, the new League of Colored Baseball Clubs was formed to act as a feeder for major league teams.

First Negro League
New York Gothams
Philadelphia Pythians
Boston Resolutes
Baltimore Lords
Pittsburgh Keystones
Cincinnati Browns
Fall City of Louisiana
Capital City of Washington

The League of Colored Baseball Clubs, suffering from financial difficulties, lasted exactly one week. At that time there were many who adopted a racist creed and were determined to chase the black man out of the baseball park—unless, of course, he paid the price of admission. One of the greatest champions of white supremacy was the irritable Adrian Constantine "Cap" Anson, manager of the Chicago White Stockings, who was one of the greatest players in baseball history. He was the Babe Ruth and John J. McGraw of his time. When his White Stockings played against Toledo, Anson saw Fleetwood Walker on the diamond and yelled, *"Get that nigger off the field."*

Anson threatened to remove his club from the field if Walker didn't leave. The Toledo management insisted that Walker would play even if the club had to get spectators out of the stands to substitute for the White Stockings. At that point Anson backed down. Some five years later when Anson found George Stovey facing his club at Newark in an exhibition game, he made the same threat. This time Stovey himself walked off and refused to play the White Stockings. Evidently this did not satisfy Anson. When Anson learned soon after that John Montgomery Ward of the Giants had planned a trade that would bring Stovey to the major leagues (thus breaking the color barrier before Jackie Robinson was even born), Anson was outraged. "There's a law against that," he bellowed. He was referring to the unwritten law resulting from a number of private agreements in professional baseball to maintain the game's "white purity."

Specifically, blacks had been barred from the National Association in 1867 and the Tri-State League in 1888. Welday Walker, then playing for Toledo in that league, said that if black players were barred they should bar black spectators as well. "The 'law,'" wrote Walker, "is a disgrace to the present age." Anson exerted pressure on Ward and convinced him to cancel the deal for Stovey and thus managed to continue the practice that kept blacks out of baseball for sixty years. Just why Anson was so strongly opposed to black players on white teams was never fully explained. His opposition to black players was a source of comment throughout every league in the country at that time. Anson's great popularity and potency in baseball circles almost single-handedly sped up the exclusion of the black man from white baseball until 1946.

In 1901 baseball history was made with the founding of the American League. That was the same year that baseball history was almost made on other frontiers. In the spring of 1901 the Baltimore Oriole club, managed by the legendary John J. McGraw, was training in Hot Springs, Arkansas, and was housed in the Eastland Hotel. One of the bellhops, Charlie Grant, had played second base for the Chicago Negro team, the Columbia Giants, in 1900. To fill their idle time, the bellhops and other hotel employees formed a baseball team. McGraw watched them play and saw immediately that Grant was of major league caliber.

Charlie Grant had been born in Cincinnati and had grown up in Cummingsville where there was a largely German population. In his youth he had learned to speak German as well as he did English. His father worked as a horse trainer at the Chester Park Track. McGraw wanted to offer Grant a contract, but knowing that there was a "law" barring black players, wondered how he was going to pull it off. Then one day, while looking at a large wall map in the lobby of the Eastland, McGraw had an idea. He called Grant over to him and told him, "Charlie, I have been trying to think of some way to sign you to the Baltimore club. I think I've got it. There's a creek on this map called Tokahama. That's going to be your name from now on. As far as anyone else is concerned, you're a full-blooded Cherokee."

Charlie Comiskey, president of the Chicago White Sox, was not taken in by McGraw's shenanigans. Comiskey said, "Somebody told me this Cherokee of McGraw's is really Grant fixed up with war paint and a bunch of feathers." Grant denied Comiskey's charge and said that his mother was a Cherokee and his father was white. He said his mother lived in Lawrence, Kansas and that McGraw could get proof that he was an Indian. McGraw backed up Grant's story, but to no avail. Grant never appeared in a regular-season major league game. He finished his ballplaying in the Negro League with the Columbia Giants in Chicago. The irony of the situation was that Comiskey himself had played against at least one black ballplayer without any complaints. Comiskey had played first base with the St. Louis Browns in 1884, when Toledo had the Walker brothers.

If there may be said to be a founding father of Negro baseball, it was Andrew "Rube" Foster, born in Calvert, Texas in 1879, the son of a Methodist minister. His first name, Andrew, might be unfamiliar to veteran baseball players, but they certainly will remember Rube Foster. One day in 1902 Foster pitched an exhibition game against the Philadelphia Athletics and their great mound star, Rube Waddell. Foster beat Waddell, and his teammates began to call him Rube, an affectionate acknowledgment that he was as capable as any pitcher around. The name stayed with him for life.

Foster was a giant, a powerful man who could pitch almost endlessly. Honus Wagner said he was "one of the greatest pitchers of all time. He was the smartest pitcher I have ever seen in all my years of baseball." He supplemented his ability with a knowledge of baseball which comes to few men. He was prepared to face any club, any batting order, no matter what its reputation. In 1905 it was reported that Foster won fifty-one games in fifty-five exhibition contests against major and minor league white teams. In Chicago he organized and pitched for one of the great Negro teams, the Leland Giants, which later became the Chicago American Giants.

When he retired as an active player Foster became the manager of the Giants and operated in the same aggressive way that John McGraw did with the Giants of the National League. In 1920 Foster helped accomplish what others had failed to do for three decades: He formed a Negro professional league. Foster won the cooperation of Ban Johnson, founder of the white American League. With Foster as president, the league had franchises in Kansas City (The Monarchs), Indianapolis (The ABCs); and Chicago, Detroit, and St. Louis (all called The Giants); plus the original American Giants and a team of traveling Cuban All Stars. Perhaps most remarkable of all, the teams in the league (except for the Cubans, who did not play home games) owned their own parks—a rare thing for any baseball league at any time.

The formation of the National Negro League led eventually to the founding of other Negro leagues: the Eastern League and the American League. There were Negro World Series as well, and players with the reputations of Satch Paige and Josh Gibson began to emerge. Rube Foster ran his league the way Ban Johnson ran the white American League—as fairly as he knew how—and like Johnson he could be tough when the occasion demanded. When Foster died in 1930 he had lived long enough to see the results of his efforts. Organized Negro baseball survived the Great Depression and flourished until the advent of black players into the major leagues.

The Negro leagues never enjoyed the stability or prosperity of their white counterparts. The reason was simple: It was an empire built on poverty. How could poor black fans finance a wealthy league? As a consequence, Negro teams were forced to play every day, traveling hundreds of miles in everything from tattered touring cars to freight trains in search of the next $500 a town would put up to match its best white players against these black intinerants. Even at their very height in the early 1940s, good black players were earning $500 a month and the leagues themselves were drawing on the average of more than 1,600 fans a game.

In 1940 Leo "Gabby" Hartnett, manager of the Chicago Cubs, said, "I'm not interested in the color of a player . . . just his ability. . . . If managers were given permission, there'd be a mad rush to sign up Negroes." In 1941 Shirley Povich of the *Washington Post* said after seeing the Washington Senators play in Florida: "There's a couple of million dollars' worth of baseball talent on the loose, ready for the big leagues, yet unsigned by any major league. There are pitchers who would win twenty games a season for any big-league club that would offer them contracts; and there are outfielders that could hit .350, infielders who could win recognition as stars, and there's at least one catcher who at this writing is probably superior to Bill Dickey: Josh Gibson.

Only one thing is keeping them out of the big leagues—the pigmentation of their skin. They happen to be colored."

October, 1942. A gorgeous Sunday afternoon; game number three of the Yankee-Cardinal World Series . . . my father and I are sitting in the center-field bleachers at the Stadium. Lefty Ernie White shuts out the Yankees 2–0. What a thrill for this kid. Joe DiMaggio hits a screamer to left center field . . . Cardinal center fielder Terry Moore makes an incredible sideways catch. He's got to be the greatest defensive outfielder my four eyes ever saw. But WAIT a minute.

A month ago in this same ballpark in a Negro National League game I saw Martin DiHigo of the Cuban All Stars do it all. Terry Moore couldn't touch him. Always there is that separation of white and black for me. My God, it drives me crazy. Studying baseball record books, reading the Sporting News *since I was ten years old, and my people cannot play in the big leagues. Why the hell am I wasting my time?*

"Three Negro baseball players will make major league history on Tuesday August 4th by trying out for positions with the Pittsburgh Pirates. The three players to be tested by the Pirates are stars in the Negro National League, and their effort to make the club has the approval of William Benswanger, president of the Pittsburgh team. Benswanger, here with his team as they met the Brooklyn Dodgers, said he told Nat Low, sports editor of the *New York Daily Worker,* that he would be willing to have the three come to Forbes Field for inspection and Low named catcher Roy Campanella, second baseman Sam Hughes of the Baltimore Elite Giants, and pitcher Dave Barnhill of the New York Cubans."

Associated Press, July 27, 1943

But the AP dispatch was a little hasty. Benswanger sent a letter to Low a few days before the tryout and informed him that he'd been a victim of pressure. The tryouts were off and thus athletes of major league caliber were again denied their rights in "the national pastime" because of the color of their skin.

Nineteen forty-two. Double-header at the Polo Grounds, Giants and Cardinals. I'm sitting behind home plate watching the greatest defensive shortstop I've ever seen. (That honor now belongs to Ozzie Smith of the St. Louis Cardinals). Martin Whitford Marion, the Richburg, South Carolina string bean who can just about play the left and right sides of the infield all by himself. Cardinal third baseman Whitey Kurowski and second baseman Frank Crespi could have stayed home. All Marion needs this day is a first baseman to throw to. In the Bronx there is a little shortstop with the Yankees named Phil Rizzuto. In Brooklyn the Dodgers have Pee Wee Reese. They play their positions superbly, but last weekend in Ruppert Stadium in Newark I saw a fantastic little shortstop with the Newark Eagles by the name of Willy Wells. God damn, that little black son of a bitch did everything Marion, Rizzuto, and Reese could do. He definitely should be on a major league club.

In 1943 Clarence "Pants" Roland, president of the Los Angeles Angels in the Pacific Coast League, announced that tryouts would be held for three Negro players: Nate Moreland, Howard Easterling, and Chet Brewer. Fourteen days later he changed his mind, apparently succumbing to the pressure of the other owners.

Spring, 1937. Lying in bed with scarlet fever. Becoming a rabid Newark Bear fan while listening to the games on WNEW as they are being broadcast by Earl Harper. What a ball club! Charlie Keller, Joe Gordon, George McQuinn, Atley Donald,

Babe Dahlgren, Joe Beggs, etc. This is a Triple-A major league ball club. I remember listening that year to the Little World Series. The Columbus Red Birds of the American Association won the first three games and then the Newark Bears come back and win four straight! The Red Birds team had such guys as Enos "Country" Slaughter, Mort Cooper, Johnny Rizzo, and Max Lanier. I am torn between rooting for the farm team of my beloved Cardinals, the Red Birds, and my new idols, the Bears, a Yankee farm club. Man, do I have the baseball bug! Maybe if I don't play in the majors I'll become a baseball writer. Hey, they don't even have black writers with the major league teams. I guess I'll have to be a doctor, lawyer, or civil servant. At least they'll let a black man do that.

Vince Devincenzi, owner of the Oakland Oaks of the Pacific Coast League, directed his manager Johnny Vergez to try out two Negro players, Chet Brewer and Olin Dial. Vergez refused. In the East Bill Veeck was trying to end the ban on black players. Veeck was operating the Milwaukee Brewers of the American Association at that time and he proposed stocking the seventh-place Philadelphia Phillies, who were up for sale, with black ballplayers. The 1943 Phillies had Bucky Harris and then "Fat" Freddie Fitzsimmons at the helm, Jim Wasdell, and the slick-fielding Babe Dahlgren at first base. But black Buck Leonard, whom Veeck had planned to sign, was a far superior initial sacker and the Phillies catchers Mickey Livingston and Andy Seminick couldn't play in the same ballpark with the great backstopper Josh Gibson. Pitching-wise, they had nothing like Satchel Paige, Leon Day, Dave Barnhill, and John Wright. The bowlegged Ray Dandrige was to be the third baseman on Veeck's team. Dandrige was the best hot-corner guy, white or black, in all of baseball. These black guys would have moved the second-division Phillies to a possible pennant and championship. When Veeck actually told Commissioner Kenesaw Mountain Landis that he was planning to buy the Phillies and fill the club with black talent, the Phillies were quickly sold to lumber magnate William Cox for half the price Veeck had been willing to pay. I guess they don't want niggers under any circumstances.

> "I have played against a Negro All-Star team that was so good, we didn't think we had an even chance against them."
>
> *Dizzy Dean*

> "I would use Negro players if given permission by those above me. It is the duty of the officials and owners to decide."
>
> *Bill McKechnie*

One beautiful day in the spring of 1938 at the Polo Grounds and I'm hanging over the wall of the bleachers in left field. I'm engaged in a conversation with Dizzy Dean, who has just been traded by the St. Louis Cardinals to the Chicago Cubs. I remember getting his autograph and then asking him about Satchel Paige, whom I'd seen pitch a week before in a Negro league game over at the Yankee Stadium. I can almost quote him verbatim: "Boy, it's too bad I couldn't throw a bucket of calcimine on him and make him white, because if he were, he'd raise hell in the majors." I then ask the big Arkansas right-hander if he would ever play with Negroes. He replies, "Hell, I play exhibitions against them. What's the difference?"

In 1945 the final season of wartime baseball saw the emergence of the black man as a major source of big-league talent. In April 1945 while the Brooklyn Dodgers were training in Bear Mountain, two black players, first baseman Dave "Showboat" Thomas and pitcher Terris McDuffie, showed up and demanded tryouts. Branch Rickey attended and felt that the players did not have major league ability. About a month and a half after the tryouts, Rickey announced the organization of a Negro league, to be named the United States League, with the entry from Brooklyn called the Brown Dodgers. This provided Rickey with the excuse to sign black players without announcing his real purpose. A committee to make a survey of "blacks in baseball" was appointed by Mayor Fiorello LaGuardia and one of those who submitted a paper on the subject was Larry MacPhail, president of the New York Yankees. His study concluded that very few Negroes were capable of playing big-league baseball, but he said that the Negro was deserving of better treatment and recommended that a few of them be admitted to organized baseball. Despite all this, Branch Rickey had already made arrangements to sign Jackie Robinson with his Brooklyn organization. This signing of Robinson was announced on October 23, 1945. Robinson was given a bonus of $3,500 and a promise of $600 a month to play with the Dodger farm club, the Montreal Royals of the International League, in 1946.

"For the first time in the history of baseball, the question of using Negro players in the major leagues will be discussed officially in the Hotel New Yorker, Friday morning. Judge Kenesaw Mountain Landis, the game's high commissioner, has put it on the agenda of the Association of the Professional Baseball Leagues."
Joe Commisky, Associated Press,
November 13, 1943

"I have seen many Negro players who should be in the major leagues. There is no room in baseball for discrimination. It is our national pastime and a game for all."
Lou Gehrig

> "I would love to hire Negro players. They are good enough for the majors."
> *Jimmy Dykes*

When Branch Rickey signed Jackie Robinson in 1945, I couldn't believe it. God damn, I said to myself, why couldn't this have happened ten years ago? I was a hell of a ballplayer; perhaps I could have made it. Now here I am, nineteen years old and a premed student at Long Island University, a sophomore. But shit, how will Robinson play a game loaded with crackers? I can't see it working out. Rickey must be out of his mind. They'll kill Jackie. My God, why can't it be 1937 instead of 1945? They missed a lot of black ballplayers who would have dominated the game.

Branch Rickey's reason in signing Robinson has frequently been misinterpreted. It was not done as a sociological ploy or because of political pressure. He signed Robinson in an attempt to win championships for the Brooklyn Dodgers. When organizations were trimming expenses during the war, Rickey was seeking new reservoirs and sources for ballplayers. Black ballplayers provided him with a plethora of untapped talent.

Robinson was a former star athlete at UCLA, Army lieutenant, and shortstop for the Kansas City Monarchs. In 1946, his rookie year with the Montreal Royals, he led the International League in batting with .349. He was voted the National League Rookie of the Year in 1947 as a first baseman with the Dodgers. He moved to second base in 1949 and won the league's Most Valuable Player award. When Rickey signed Robinson there were many who thought that black baseball players were just beginning to develop. But blacks had for many years watched some great talent displayed in the Negro leagues which, although somewhat disorganized, still provided some good paydays for many of the country's best black athletes.

Going back, one of the original black clubs that the partici-
pants found to be more fun than money was the Cuban Giants.
The group was led by a hotel headwaiter by the name of Frank
Thompson. The club consisted of members of the staff of the
Argyle Hotel in Babylon, Long Island. The Cuban Giants' moniker was misleading because there wasn't a Cuban to be found in
the bunch. The Cuban Giants had two of the best ballplayers active at the time: Shep Trusty, top black pitcher of the 1880s, and
Sol White, a tremendous long-ball hitter. In their first professional year (1881), a year that saw them paid wages equivalent
to those to be had by the help in a first-class hotel, they beat
Bridgeport, Connecticut, the Eastern League champions. This
established them as a strong attraction.

They beat Cincinnati and Indianapolis in the International
League in 1887 and threw a scare into many other white major
league clubs they played. Stimulated by the success of the
Giants, "Cuban" and "Giant" teams of all sorts came into existence, almost all of them managed and organized by white
promoters attempting to take advantage of the success of the
Cuban Giant team. There were the Elite Giants, the Mohawk
Giants, the Cuban X Giants, the Genuine Cuban Giants, the
Leland Giants, the Lincoln Giants of Lincoln, Nebraska, and the
Brooklyn Royal Giants. In order to make more than a meager
living out of the game, the black players had to play all year round
in Central and South America, in Cuba, in Mexico, and in other
places where black pigmentation did not mark a man as second
class. It was in these locations that the black population would
turn out in large numbers and pack the ballpark.

Some of the ballplayers were better than those playing
white baseball. For instance, just before World War I there was
Frank Wickware, a long, reed-thin, right-handed fireballing
black pitcher from Coffeyville, Kansas, who was nicknamed
"The Red Ant" because his body was devoid of fat and meat.
While pitching for the Mohawk Giants against a barnstorming

major league squad called the Walter Johnson All-Stars, Wickware beat them and struck out seventeen of his opponents.

Around that time in New York City, one of the best black teams in the United States played at Olympic Field at 138th and Fifth Avenue. The team was the Lincoln Giants, who had given up Nebraska as their home base. At that time the Lincoln Giants had two of the greatest pitchers extant: Cyclone Joe Williams and Ad Langford. Both of them faced and beat most of the leading white clubs in the major leagues. There were many other great black players around at that time. A forerunner of the peerless Josh Gibson was the fearless Buddy Petway. He was throwing from a crouch long before any white catcher. Then there was Henry "Pop" Lloyd from Palatka, Florida, a shortstop who some say was equal or superior to Honus Wagner. He was a powerful hitter, and as a fielder he had no rival. He possessed enormous hands that could engulf a ground ball, and it was said that he threw like a cannon.

Between World Wars I and II and through the Depression, organized black teams played full schedules in their own leagues despite substandard wages, abominable playing conditions, and poor transportation. The black man played ball in preference to taking the miserable jobs offered him elsewhere. There were many big stars in the black leagues who could have made it in the majors and earned five-figure salaries if given the chance. There was Josh Gibson of the Pittsburgh Crawfords. He certainly could have made it. Black ballplayers said he could hit the ball a mile. And there was Cool Papa Bell of the St. Louis Stars, an outfielder as speedy and graceful as Tris Speaker. There was first baseman Buck Leonard, who many call the black Lou Gehrig; and of course, there was pitcher Leroy "Satchel" Paige, who did for black baseball what Babe Ruth did for white baseball. Satch didn't actually put black baseball into a class with the major leagues, but he made it a lot easier for the black players to demand better salaries and playing conditions.

The lack of official records was one price black ballplayers had to pay. Even though everyone knew, for example, that Josh Gibson had hit many more home runs in a season than Babe Ruth had, documentation was nebulous. There were those who watched Gibson hit four home runs out of Griffith Stadium in one game, bur there were no record bureaus to verify that it really happened. Many spectators who saw them all might agree that Satchel Paige, Chet Brewer, or Bullet Joe Rogan could throw "small baseballs" like Bob Feller or Walter Johnson, yet the strikeouts were not set down anywhere. One could perhaps find a newspaper account somewhere talking about lefty John Donaldson of the Chicago Giants . . . twenty-three strikeouts in a single game. But if these records were not in the "white man's book," they did not count.

Despite disallowing blacks to play in the majors at that time, organized baseball ultimately has been shamed into admitting some of those great black ballplayers to their Hall of Fame in Cooperstown. This came about after Ted Williams, in accepting his own election to the Hall, strongly criticized the "stuffed shirts" attending the ceremony by telling them that black players should be admitted. The first thought by the baseball moguls was to isolate the black heroes in a "special" section. Fortunately the baseball brass suffered either sudden shame or good sense, or maybe they felt the pressure of public dismay and agreed to accept the blacks on an equal scale with the whites—not many of whom, it must be stated here, were any more than just equal to the best of the black players.

You had Buck Leonard, first baseman of the Homestead Grays, who perhaps was a better fielder at his position than Hal Chase or George Sisler—and he definitely was a harder hitter than those two. Willy Wells of the Newark Eagles probably was just as good as Marty Marion, Pee Wee Reese, or Phil Rizzuto. Oscar Charleston of the Pittsburgh Crawfords would almost certainly rank with Joe DiMaggio or Terry Moore in center field.

But these players never got a chance to prove their skills in the white major leagues.

Nineteen forty-two. The All-Star Game, a twi-nighter at the Polo Grounds. Two fantastic squads. Mort Cooper got bombed for three runs in the first inning . . . this coming about as a result of a lead-off homer by American League shortstop Lou Boudreau, a double to right field by Tommy Henrich, and a home run by Rudy York. While sitting behind home plate with my late friends George Vaz and Archie Cruz, I say to myself, "This is the greatest array of stars I have ever seen." Then I recall that I had attended the Negro All-Star game in Chicago's Comiskey Park that year. These "niggers" had teams comparable if not superior to the clubs I had seen at the Polo Grounds. Guys like Sam Jethroe, Josh Gibson, Buck Leonard, Satchel Paige, Willard Brown, and Jim West, a first baseman who by far was the best fielding initial sacker I'd ever seen. God, those guys should be in the major leagues . . . right now!

BUCK LEONARD

At the peak of his career, Buck Leonard was a svelte 5-foot-10, 185-pounder who frequently batted cleanup behind the more publicized Josh Gibson. He dug into the batter's box with a certain defiance, crouching menacingly in a slightly open stance. From that posture Buck pulled the ball with power and consistency. Many say that Buck Leonard, first baseman of the Homestead Grays, was perhaps as good a fielder at his position as the legendary Hal Chase, and he was surely a stronger hitter.

Buck Leonard performed for the Homestead Grays and the Brooklyn Royal Giants from 1933 to 1950. His best years in the

Negro National League were 1941 and 1942. In 1941 he batted .392 and led the league at bat. The following year he hit forty-two home runs.

Born in Rocky Mount, North Carolina, in 1907, he lived in a place called Little Raleigh. He remembered that he started following baseball when they erected the City Park Municipal Stadium near his house. When he got out of school in 1921 he went to work at a mill and made stockings. Then he shined shoes at the railroad station.

Leonard started with the Homestead Grays in 1934. He was paid $125 a month. By 1941 he was making $175 a month plus 75 cents a day eating expenses. In 1942 his pay was upped to $1,000 a month. His best pay was in 1948; he made $10,000 that year, and that was for summer *and* winter games. Batting champ on the Grays behind Josh Gibson, he and Josh formed the most powerful hitting duo in black baseball, a Babe Ruth–Lou Gehrig combination. From 1937 to 1945, Leonard's Grays won nine straight pennants.

In 1922 he played semi-pro ball around Rocky Mount and also worked at the Atlantic Coast Line Railroad shop for nine years. He played on a team called the Black Swans and another one called the Elks Team. They played in Norfolk, Newport News, Wilson; and all around Raleigh, Durham, and Winston-Salem. In 1933 he went to Portsmouth, Virginia and played with a team called the Firefighters.

Leonard learned how to play first base from Ben Taylor, whom he calls the greatest first baseman in black history. Taylor had a team in Baltimore called the Baltimore Stars. Leonard's Firefighters played the Stars in 1933 and afterward Taylor asked him to join the team. He did, and went to Winston-Salem, Charlotte, and Statesville. Buck said it was a rough trip and he almost starved to death. The rest of the 1933 season Leonard played with the Brooklyn Royal Giants. In 1934 he joined Cum Posey's Homestead Grays, where he remained for seventeen years.

"Buck Leonard was as smooth a first baseman as I ever saw. In those days the first basemen on a team in the Negro League often played the clown. They had a funny way of catching the ball so the fans would laugh, but Leonard was strictly baseball: a great glove, a hell of a hitter, and he drove in runs. Buck Leonard was just as good as Hal Chase."

Eddie Gotlieb

"Satchel Paige and Josh Gibson got more publicity in the Negro League, but Buck Leonard was just as good."

Monte Irvin

BUCK LEONARD: It was tough playing in the Negro leagues. A lot of riding, a lot of playing. Some seasons we would play 210 ball games. You're riding every day, playing in different towns. No air conditioning. Meals were bad. When I first started playing we were getting 60 cents a day on which to eat and we stayed in rooming houses. You know we couldn't stay in the good hotels. Then they started giving us 75 cents a day to eat on. At that time (1933, 1934, 1935) you could eat for 60 cents a day, but it was tough, and then they raised it to 75 cents a day, and then $1. When I stopped playing baseball in 1950, we were getting $2 a day for meal money. Of course, conditions then were much better in those days. In 1943, during the Second World War when people couldn't get gasoline to travel, our salaries went up, and from 1943 to 1950 things were much better.

When I was playing in the Negro leagues I always thought that eventually blacks would be playing in the major leagues, but just when, I didn't know. We felt we should have been in the major leagues. Most of us knew we could have made it in the majors, but since they decided not to have us, we just made ourselves content playing in our own league. We had a Negro National League, a Negro American League. Six teams in each league and in September at the end of the season we had the Black World Series. We had a lot of fun and we enjoyed playing. We really loved the game. I played with the Homestead Grays for seventeen years. I played professional baseball for twenty-three years. I started playing sandlot baseball down home in Rocky Mount, North Carolina, until 1933. I joined the Baltimore Stars, managed by Ben Taylor, the old first baseman. Then I came to New York and played with the Brooklyn Royal Giants. Dick Redding was the manager. Then in 1934 I went to the Homestead Grays and played there until 1950, the year the club broke up. Later I went to Mexico and played five years on a Mexican team. I would play in the U.S. during the summer with the Homestead Grays, then I would go to Cuba, Puerto Rico, Venezuela, and Mexico and play during the winter. I played twenty-three winters and twenty-three summers of baseball. I was in twelve All-Star games in Chicago.

"Buck had a real quick bat—you couldn't get a fast ball by him, and he hit the curve real well, too. If he was hitting behind Gibson, you could sort of pitch around him, try to keep the ball away from him and make him hit at an off-speed pitch. He was strictly a pull hitter and he had about as much power as Ted Kluszewski. . . . He was major league all the way. He was one of the best hitters I've ever seen."
Roy Campanella

When you play for twenty-three years, you know, you have many thrills. I guess my biggest one was when my club, the Birmingham Black Barons, was in the Negro World Series in 1948. That was our greatest team. Josh Gibson wasn't with us.

He was dead. (Josh Gibson died January 20, 1947, in Pittsburgh, Pennsylvania.) We had Luke Easter and Roy Welmaker (who both went to the Cleveland Indians) and Luis Marquez. Marquez went up to the Boston Braves.

At that time Willie Mays was playing with the Birmingham Black Barons. He was about fifteen. He could run and he could throw. His hitting wasn't so good, because at that time he couldn't hit a curve ball. In 1941 I hit .392 to lead the Negro National League in batting. In 1942 I hit forty-two homers, the most I ever hit in one season. When I joined the Grays they were a Pittsburgh-based team. We started playing in Washington in 1937. We played our games in Griffith Stadium in Washington when the Senators were on the road and in Forbes Field in Pittsburgh when the Pirates were away. For awhile we used a colored park in Pittsburgh called Greenlee Field. The stands didn't have a top on it and you know how hot it could get in the sun!

When the Dodgers signed Jackie Robinson we didn't think he was that good, but you can't always tell about a ballplayer. Sometimes you look at a guy and don't think that much of him. Then he turns into one hell of a ballplayer. But Jackie had the education and that's what they were looking for as the first black.

There were other guys we thought were better, but they got the right man after all. When Jackie was signed, they were talking about bringing me, Willy Wells, Lennie Pearson, and Cool Papa Bell up, but they were looking for younger players, players they could depend upon for at least five years. In 1952, when I was in Mexico, Bill Veeck, who was with the St. Louis Browns—Satchel Paige was with them at the time—called me and asked me whether I would like to join the team in spring training in California. I told them no. Hell, I was forty-five years old then. My legs were gone. Who was I fooling! I knew I couldn't play baseball every day, and I didn't even want to try it.

Buck Leonard was elected to the Hall of Fame in 1972.

JOSH GIBSON

Josh Gibson was born in Buena Vista, Georgia on December 21, 1911. When he was twelve his family migrated to Pittsburgh, Pennsylvania. At that time, swimming was his number-one interest. He won many medals from various pools in the neighborhood. At the age of sixteen he played his first game of baseball.

> "I'd name Josh Gibson one of the greatest catchers in the history of baseball. He does everything well."
> *Dolph Camilli*

Playing with a uniformed ball club, the Gimbels A.C., Gibson dropped out of school after the ninth grade and went to work in a factory that made air brakes. At eighteen, Josh was 6-foot-1 and he weighed 215 pounds. He had tremendous arms, a barrel chest, and a very slim waist. In 1929 and 1930 he caught for the Crawford Colored Giants of Pittsburgh, a semi-pro team. The Crawfords played other semi-pro teams in Pittsburgh and environs for a few dollars a game. The games attracted big crowds, which were readily becoming aware of Gibson's tremendous hitting. In July 1930, in an exhibition between the Kansas City Monarchs and the Homestead Grays, Buck Ewing, the catcher for the Grays, suffered a split finger and could not continue. Josh was watching the game from the stands and was asked if he would like to catch. He accepted. From that night on, he became a regular on the Grays. Roy Campanella, no mean catcher and hitter himself, said, "Knowing Josh Gibson and knowing Hank Aaron and playing against him too, I think Josh was the greatest home-run hitter I ever saw. Now it's true, nobody has ever counted the home runs this man has hit, but I'll say one thing. I'll put him with anybody, not taking anything away from Babe Ruth. I think Josh Gibson is the greatest home-run hitter that ever lived."

In 1931, as an established star with the Homestead Grays, Josh was credited with seventy-five home runs as the team barnstormed through New York State. In 1932 Satchel Paige joined Gus Greenlee's Pittsburgh Crawfords and for the next five years, formed one of the greatest batteries in baseball with

"I played ball on the same team with Josh for nine years. I hit third, he hit fourth. Sometimes I would hit fourth and he would hit third, according to who was doing the better batting at the time. If I was in a slump I would move down a little and he would move up to third and that's the way we rotated. But in my opinion, Josh was one of the greatest ballplayers of all time. He wasn't the greatest catcher, so to speak, but he was one of the greatest hitters. So far as catching and handling pitchers, he wasn't so sharp at that. We had several guys who were a little better— Biz Mackey and Roy Campanella. They were better in handling pitchers and catching pop flies around home plate. But when it came to running and hitting and throwing, I don't know anybody that could beat him. Josh was the most powerful hitter we had in the Negro leagues. I saw him hit one out of Yankee Stadium. At the Polo Grounds I saw him hit one between the upper deck and the roof. It hit an elevated train track outside the park. Josh hit seventy to seventy-two home runs in one year. In 1939 he hit more home runs in Griffith Stadium than all the right-handed hitters in the American League combined."

Buck Leonard

Josh Gibson. Near the end of the 1936 season Josh returned to the Homestead Grays. The powerful Gray ball club was the strongest in Negro baseball. For the next two years the combination of Gibson's hitting, along with power from sluggers like Buck Leonard, Sam Bankhead, and Vic Harris, helped the Grays to several successive championships. But by this time, Josh Gibson, who for twelve years had been one of the mainstays of black baseball, had developed a fondness for alcohol. In the final five years he was suspended occasionally by manager Cum Posey for "overindulgence."

"Josh Gibson was black and they wouldn't let him play in the major leagues. If they had ever let him play in a small place like the old Ebbets Field or the old Fenway Park, Josh Gibson would have forced baseball to rewrite the rules. He was, at the minimum, two Yogi Berras."
Bill Veeck

One day in January of 1943 Josh blacked out and lay in a coma in a Pittsburgh hospital. He had suffered from recurring headaches for quite some time. The doctors diagnosed it as a brain tumor but Gibson was afraid to let the doctors operate. Shortly thereafter he signed himself out, and despite his ailment, he returned to baseball, leading the Negro League in batting in 1945 and 1946. In 1946 Gibson's headaches and blackouts increased in frequency and severity and he started to drink more heavily. Gibson died on January 20, 1947 in Pittsburgh, Pennsylvania, one year after Jackie Robinson had broken the baseball color barrier at Montreal and a few months before Robinson would become the first black in modern major league baseball since the Walker brothers, Moses and Welday, in 1884.

Josh Gibson was elected to the Baseball Hall of Fame in 1972.

JAMES "COOL PAPA" BELL

James Thomas Bell was born May 17, 1903 in Starksville, Mississippi. As to his career, there were no records kept. He spent twenty-nine years in the Negro leagues, the California winter league, the Mexican league, and the Dominican Republic. His best year was 1933, when he stole 175 bases in an estimated 200-game season. He hit .480 one year; no other batting records are available. Originally a right-handed batter, he taught himself to become a switch hitter.

"Cool Papa" Bell was the black Willie Keeler at bat and the black Tris Speaker in center field."
Eddie Gotlieb

"COOL PAPA" BELL: When I played it was good, because baseball was my life at the time. I thought it was a great thing for me to play and travel because I always wanted to travel. We were happy when we were playing. We didn't regret that the doors were not open to black players at the time, but I'm glad it's been open for the black boys from now on. I didn't make a lot of money—wasn't much money then—but you could do more with the money we were making then. Sometimes it was tough traveling. When you first got started you had to make small towns where the trains didn't even stop, so we had to take buses. We traveled from one town to another and rested overnight. Sometimes we went 100 to 150 miles. Sometimes we would get there just in time to start the game.

I started playing Negro ball in 1922 with the St. Louis Stars. I played ten years there, from '22 through '31. I left there and went to the Detroit Senators in 1932. That team was owned by Cum Posey, as was the Homestead Grays; so the Detroit Senators folded but they kept about five players for the Grays. We played there for a month and a half and they took us off salary. As a result, I finished the season with the Kansas City Monarchs. In 1933 I went to the Pittsburgh Crawfords where I played until '36. In 1937 I played in Santo Domingo. I helped win the championship down there for Trujillo. We played under the name of the Trujillo All-Stars. From '38 to '41 I played in Mexico. In '42 I played with the Chicago American Giants and from '43 to '46 I played with the Homestead Grays. From '48 to '50 I managed the farm team of the Monarchs. That was my last year in baseball.

When I first started playing ball, two black guys were my idols: Oscar Charleston, a great outfielder, and Jimmy Lyons, a fine outfielder and a great base runner. Oscar Charleston was the greatest center fielder, they say. Before him they say there was a guy named Spottswood Poles, but after him they say that Charleston was the greatest. I started out as a pitcher in Negro baseball, and then I moved to the outfield. I went to Indianapolis in 1922 and Oscar Charleston was there. They hit baseballs to me and Charleston and I could go farther than he could to get the ball. (I didn't have his experience because I hadn't played the outfield like he did, but I could go farther because I was faster.) In Chicago they had me run against Jimmy Lyons when he was supposed to be the fastest man alive, and I beat him.

"I was only nineteen and they thought I'd be afraid of big crowds . . . I took it so cool, they began to call me 'Cool.' But that wasn't enough—they added 'Papa' to it."
James "Cool Papa" Bell

"Cool Papa" Bell was the fastest thing I ever saw on a baseball field. I roomed with him for five years. When I knew Bell he was in the evening of his career, but he could still fly."
Buck Leonard

Around 1938. The New York Giants and St. Louis Cardinals at the Polo Grounds. Dick Coffman pitching for the Giants. Don Gutteridge, St. Louis third baseman, pulls one down the left-field line. God, that son of a bitch can run! Fastest guy I've ever seen in a baseball uniform. But I'd forgotten about the Negro National League game I saw in this same park two weeks ago. James "Cool Papa" Bell., St. Louis Stars' outfielder—hell, he can walk faster than Gutteridge can run.

When I became a regular outfielder, I played twenty-seven years there and two as a pitcher. I played twenty-nine summer seasons and twenty-one winter seasons of baseball. I played heads-up baseball. I never would settle for first base. I'd go to second, then third, then home. I was an aggressive ballplayer. I tried to do a little more than most ballplayers.

In those early years of Negro baseball, only once was I approached by a major league team. It was in 1935 when we played Earle Mack's (son of Connie Mack, who owned the Philadelphia Athletics) team in Mexico City and they had Rogers Hornsby, Doc Cramer, Heinie Manush, Jimmy Foxx, Max Bishop, and a lot of those guys playing. There was a great big park in Mexico City, and in this particular game Hornsby, his first time up, hit a ball over the left-field fence for a home run. The next time he came up he hit a ball to deep center over my head and I ran a long way and caught the ball. I was all over the outfield that day.

Hornsby said to me, "Lefty"—that's what he called me— "how did you catch that ball?" I told him I just ran back and caught it. And he said that was the hardest ball he'd ever hit in baseball and I had to catch it. Earle Mack said to me, "I want to congratulate you. If the doors were open to black ballplayers, you'd be the first one I'd get." He said, "I could afford to pay you $75,000 a year." I said, "Thank you," and he replied, "Maybe that time will come some day."

When I first came up, I felt a black man would never play in the majors, but as the years went by I felt that some day it would happen. We used to see scouts at the Negro league games, but those scouts used to say, "I couldn't find anyone." They would say, "If we could find one who could play major league ball, we would hire him." But they were never honest with us about why they would not allow us to play. Blacks could play if given the opportunity.

Jackie Robinson maybe did not know about this, but when we played the Kansas City Monarchs, the team Jackie was with, in Delaware in 1945, I was with the Homestead Grays. Frank Duncan, the Kansas City manager, came to me and asked me to do something for him, more specifically something for the future of the black ballplayer. He said, "This fall sometime or in the winter when the season is over, Jackie Robinson will be signed into organized baseball. He wants to go up as a shortstop. We want him to play second, third, first, or the outfield." I was the kind of guy who could hit the ball to any field nine out of ten times, and Duncan said, "I want you to hit the ball to Jackie's right, deep at shortstop. He doesn't go over there too well and he pivots poorly." The first two times up I hit that ball over there and Jackie caught the ball in the "hole" but he didn't backhand the ball. You're supposed to backhand the ball if you can't get in front of it. He caught the ball and had to take two steps before he threw, and I beat both of those plays out.

The next two times up I walked. I stole four bases that night trying to confuse him. So I would go into the bag and put one foot up for him to see. He'd reach for it, I would jerk it back and slide the other one over the base, reach my hand back, slide, and step over his hand. These are the kinds of tricks he did in the majors. He learned them from me. I told him, "Jackie, shortstop is not your position." So after that he thought about it and they moved him over to second base. Jackie was satisfied, and what a great job he did.

Maury Wills was already stealing bases but I talked to him before he broke the record. I told him when he was on the bases to tell the batters to step back in the batters' box, make the catcher back up a little bit. That would give him about two or three more steps. Wills said he didn't think about that. But he broke the record that day.

Funny, but I don't have any regrets about not playing in the majors. At that time the doors were not open not only in baseball, but other avenues that we couldn't enter. They say that I was born too soon. I say the doors were opened up too late.

James "Cool Papa" Bell became the fifth black in the Hall of Fame when he was selected in 1974. He died on March 2, 1991, in St. Louis.

JUDY JOHNSON

A lean 5-foot, 11-1/2-inch 145-pounder, William J. "Judy" Johnson played in the Negro leagues from 1920 until 1938 with the Hilldale Daisies, the Homestead Grays, the Darby Daisies, and the Pittsburgh Crawfords. For the seven years that statistics were kept in the Negro leagues, Johnson averaged in the mid-.340s and was considered the best fielding third baseman in the Negro leagues. They called him the black Pie Traynor. Judy Johnson signed with the Hilldale Club in 1922 for $135 a month, the average pay in the Negro leagues at that time.

JUDY JOHNSON: Around 1920 I went to Philadelphia to play semi-pro ball and there was an old-time player named Judy Gans on the team. He said I looked so much like him I could be his son. So they started calling me Judy. The first time we ever played in Connie Mack stadium, my daddy came to watch me and told me that it would happen one day. And I told him he was having pipe dreams. The question of playing in the big leagues never occurred to me until I was twenty or so and playing ball already. Then it occurred to me that I should be playing. Often I've wished I could've played at the time Jackie Robinson came up. I feel as though I could've given something to help my race along.

When I was with the Grays, to get into spring training from Pittsburgh to Hot Springs we went eighteen men in two cars. It was tough. We'd always try to hit a big city. In the little, small places we couldn't even use a rest room. I was lucky. I made $500 a month a few years, and you could make nearly as much barnstorming or playing winter ball. On the Hilldale club we didn't travel too much, just around Pennsylvania. With Hilldale, I was home practically every evening.

I've been asked many times what the caliber of play was in the Negro leagues. Day in, day out, I would say the leagues were not of major league quality. But you could easily pick a team of black players who could beat the hell out of the white major leagues any day. Overall I would say that most of the Negro teams were of Triple-A quality. My biggest thrill playing in the Negro leagues was when we played and beat major league All-Stars. It gave us confidence that our ability was equal to theirs.

I remember the first big-league pitcher I ever faced was Bullet Joe Bush. This was back in 1922. I was playing with Hilldale, and we were playing Earle Mack's All-Stars. Bush was fresh from a twenty-six-game win season with the pennant-winning Yankees. Man, we hit him good. We also used to give A's right-hander George Earnshaw fits on those barnstorming trips. You know, the average player on the Crawfords could have played big-league ball. There was one guy who, if it boiled down to being the first black in the major leagues in my time, I would say it would have to be Martin DiHigo. He was the greatest all-around ballplayer I ever saw.

"If Judy were only white, he could name his price."

Connie Mack

Playing conditions were rough in the Negro leagues. I remember a nonstop bus tour from Chicago to Philadelphia after a double-header, almost a thousand miles of sodas; sandwiches for breakfast, lunch, and dinner. When we finally pulled into Philadelphia everyone was totally exhausted, but we played a double-header in Connie Mack Stadium.

I was a good friend of Connie Mack, owner of the Philadelphia Athletics. One day I asked him why he didn't sign a black player. He told me, "There were too many of you to go in. It would have taken too many jobs away from the white boys." It was rumored that in 1929 when the Athletics played the Chicago Cubs in the World Series, they were short of players. It was said that Mack was thinking about signing two black players, Raleigh "Biz" Mackey and Luis Santop.

In March, 1975, Judy Johnson was elected to the Baseball Hall of Fame. He died June 19, 1989, in Washington, D.C.

The following is a list of Negro League stars who, in the opinion of the black ballplayers I polled, were the best at their positions in the Negro leagues.

FIRST BASE:
WALTER "BUCK" LEONARD
HOMESTEAD GRAYS
Leonard was a cross between Lou Gehrig and Hal Chase. A fancy fielder and a powerful hitter, he was steady, smooth, smart, and consistently batted about .300.

SECOND BASE:
ELWOOD "BINGO" DE MOSS
CHICAGO AMERICAN GIANTS

De Moss was a finished performer of the Charles Gehringer type: fast, intelligent, a good hitter, and a master of the double play. Old-timers recall that he fielded his position with grace and ease. Unlike Gehringer, however, he was a "holler guy;" a field general.

THIRD BASE:
JUDY JOHNSON
PITTSBURGH CRAWFORDS

One of Negro baseball's most fabulous players. He was equally adept at fielding balls to his right and left; was sure-handed on bunts, and owned a strong arm.

SHORTSTOP:
JOHN HENRY "POP" LLOYD
LINCOLN GIANTS

Lloyd was big for a shortstop at 5-foot-11, 180 pounds. He ranged all over the field. Had long arms and big hands and handled many balls that other shortstops could not reach. He had tremendous presence at the plate and has been often compared to Honus Wagner.

LEFT FIELD:
PETE HILL
CHICAGO AMERICAN GIANTS

Called by Cum Posey "the most consistent hitter of his time," he hit both left-handed and right-handed equally well. He was the backbone, year in and year out, of the great ball clubs.

CENTER FIELD:
OSCAR CHARLESTON
PITTSBURGH CRAWFORDS

No other center-fielder in Negro baseball matched Oscar Charleston and old-timers say it is subject to debate whether Tris Speaker, Willie Mays, Joe DiMaggio, and Terry Moore were his superiors. He was a marvelous defensive outfielder who combined hitting ability with tremendous speed and a powerful throwing arm.

RIGHT FIELD:
CRISTOBAL TORRIENTI
CHICAGO AMERICAN GIANTS

A Cuban who stood 5-feet-10 and weighed 190 pounds. A strong left-handed pull hitter with a powerful throwing arm. Jelly Gardner, his teammate on the American Giants, said, "A New York Giant scout would have signed him except for the fact that he had kinky hair."

CATCHER:
JOSH GIBSON
HOMESTEAD GRAYS, PITTSBURGH CRAWFORDS

Powerful hitting backstop. Perhaps one of the strongest men in all baseball at the time he was playing. He hit baseballs legendary distances.

CATCHER:
RALEIGH "BIZ" MACKEY
NEWARK EAGLES

Big, strong, and relatively fast, he was a switch-hitter with above-average power. Defensively a fine handler of pitchers, and possessed of an accurate and powerful throwing arm.

PITCHER:

JOHN DONALDSON
CHICAGO GIANTS

One of the finest southpaws in Negro baseball; possessing speed, a good changeup, an assortment of curves, and good control. An excellent fielder and batter, too.

PITCHER:

WILBUR "BULLET" ROGAN
KANSAS CITY MONARCHS

One of the most versatile black ballplayers that ever played the game. He had a lightning-fast ball as a hurler with the Monarchs. Rogan often pitched and played three or four other positions in one game.

PITCHER:

CHET BREWER
KANSAS CITY MONARCHS

Almost a double for Satchel Paige; extremely fast, and he had a wicked curve.

And in my All-Star book, Satchel Paige will always belong right there on the mound.

EDDIE GOTTLIEB

Eddie Gottlieb has had one of the most extensive and varied careers of anyone in American sports. He was the founder and coach of the Philadelphia SPHAs, which won seven professional basketball championships in fourteen years from the late 1920s to the early 1940s. He coached the Philadelphia Warriors to the 1946–47 NBA championship, the first year of the team's existence. The Warriors repeated in 1956. In 1962 he sold the team but maintained his active link with the NBA by continuing to serve as chairman of the NBA Rules Committee, schedule maker of the NBA, and Consultant to the Commissioner. In 1972 he was elected to the Naismith Basketball Hall of Fame and was inducted in April, 1973.

For decades he was connected with Negro professional baseball as owner and promoter, and he was appointed to a blue-ribbon committee by Baseball Commissioner Bowie Kuhn to select worthy black players to the Baseball Hall of Fame.

EDDIE GOTTLIEB: In the thirties Gus Greenlee got the idea of staging some four-team double-headers at Yankee Stadium. The first of the four-team double-headers in June 1932 had the Pittsburgh Crawfords against the Philadelphia Stars and the Chicago American Giants against the New York Black Yankees. The Crawfords and the Stars played a 1–1 tie with Slim Jones of the Stars pitching against Satchel Paige of the Crawfords.

An interesting feature of that first game is that it started raining on Friday, it rained all day Saturday, and Sunday morning when I got out of bed in Philadelphia, it was still raining. You would never think a game could be played that day. We got into the cars and buses, players and all. We drove to New York and it rained all the way down the highway—it was really pouring. When we got out of the Holland Tunnel, the rain had stopped. We went to the ballpark—it was still very cloudy and threatening—and tried to figure out whether to open the gates or not. We finally decided we would and see what happened.

At about twelve thirty the people started coming, and they stormed the gates, knocking over ticket boxes. We were not really prepared for this and we did not have enough ticket-takers. We immediately put everybody to work who could sell tickets. We wound up with about 20,000 people in spite of everything. Several weeks later, when we repeated the same double-header, we had exactly the same conditions. It rained Friday, Saturday, and again on Sunday morning. We played anyway and had just about 24,000 people again, so it was very successful. Also involved in these promotions was Nat Strong, who was the biggest booking agent in the East. He had control of the New York Black Yankees.

I would say the grade of baseball played in the Negro National Leagues at that time was equal to Double-A or Triple-A baseball. This was verified by some of the people connected with big-league baseball. (We played in the big-league parks, and that's what they said.) Looking back years later, when the black player started to go into the major leagues we really discovered we were playing major league ball because we had more players of major league caliber probably than a lot of players on the major league teams.

In the beginning we didn't have too much trouble renting the parks. We originally started at the Yankee Stadium. We didn't play at the Polo Grounds or Ebbets Field. Gus Greenlee made the original arrangements. I don't think he had much difficulty, but as we started playing game to game, they started raising our rent. It got to the point that after a couple of years we weren't drawing as well as we were at the beginning and the rent got so high that it was impossible for us to continue playing. So Greenlee said one year, "We'll stop playing at Yankee Stadium. We'll play at Randall's Island." Well, Randall's Island was a flop! The people wouldn't sit out in the sun and the discomfort when they could sit in the shade at Yankee Stadium.

After the season was over I went back to Yankee Stadium and talked to Ed Barrow. I asked him if we could come to some kind of compromise. We came to an agreement and Barrow drew up a new lease. Later we started playing at the Polo Grounds, too, because we couldn't get all the dates we wanted at the Stadium. Then we played some games at Ebbets Field in Brooklyn, which turned out to be a failure. We felt it wouldn't be successful because the black population around Ebbets Field was not like it was around the Polo Grounds and Yankee Stadium. And what black population there was around Ebbets Field didn't live as close to the field as they did in Manhattan.

In those days, the percentage of white patrons at Negro games was very small. But prior to that, at the Hilldale Club in Philadelphia, the percentage of white patrons was very big. I had a semi-pro team that played against the Lincoln Giants at the Catholic Protectory. The percentage of whites was about 80 percent. I guess it all depended on what neighborhood we were in. Later on when we played the All-Star games, like the Satchel Paige Stars against the Bob Feller Stars, we drew 50,000 to 60,000 people for the games. There the white population was about 15 percent.

Prior to the Negro National League games, the only game involving black players that was ever seen in Yankee Stadium was between the Lincoln Giants and the Baltimore Black Sox for the benefit of the Pullman porters. I think the rental that was asked to play those games and the reluctance of the teams' owners kept the teams away, but later when we showed how successful it could become and the rent became reasonable, we were able to put on games all over the circuit, like Griffith Stadium in Washington and Shibe Park in Philadelphia. The first black team that had a regular park was the Kansas City Monarchs. They played in Muehlenbach Park and they outdrew Kansas City of the American Association, their white counterparts.

Satch Paige was without a doubt the greatest drawing attraction in Negro baseball. He was like Babe Ruth. What magnetism he had! I think of the first time I brought Satch into Philadelphia with the Monarchs in the early thirties. We didn't play in a big-league park at that time. We played in a small park and I sold tickets myself. Later on I booked him into Shibe Park with the Monarchs and the Philadelphia Stars. There we drew about 30,000 people.

Earlier, when Gus Greenlee started the Pittsburgh Crawfords, he had Satchel Paige, Josh Gibson, Buck Leonard, and Ted Page. One hell of a team, with Satch as his main attraction. Greenlee asked me to book his club. His main competition at that time in Pittsburgh were the Homestead Grays. I spoke to promoter Nat Strong in New York, and he said that if I would handle them during the week, he would take them on Sundays.

"Some of the clubs I was on are a legend. When you mention baseball clubs over the years, among the first names that come up are the Homestead Grays and the Pittsburgh Crawfords. Why do they mention these teams? Because they had superstars. In my thinking and from what I have seen of the Yankees of 1927 or the St. Louis Cardinals of 1934—the Gashouse Gang, as they called themselves—I would say that the Pittsburgh Crawfords or the Homestead Grays would have been just as good or better than these two clubs. Guys like Josh Gibson, Satch Paige, Oscar Charleston, Judy Johnson, Rap Dixon, Jimmy Crutchfield, and others, compared with anybody on the '27 Yankees and the '34 Cardinals."

Ted Page
Homestead Grays, Pittsburgh Crawfords

We started the Crawfords playing twi-night ball from Monday through Friday. I guaranteed that Satch would pitch an inning or possibly three. Satch would come out every day for those twi-night games. He would pitch three innings a day, and in most cases strike out three men on nine or ten pitches. On the weekends Paige would come over to New York and pitch nine innings against the Bushwicks or whatever teams were available. Satch threw a "pea" ball—that's how fast he was—he made the ball look that small. The only trouble with Satch was times when he didn't appear. You would never know what had happened to him. He would sometimes get caught speeding or he would miss a plane.

On one tour I had Oscar Charleston, who was playing and managing for the Chicago Stars, and we were going against the Indianapolis Clowns. We went out on a tour for twenty-nine or thirty days, and Charleston slept in the room with Satchel to make sure that he didn't get away. That was his job. In 1954, after Satch was out of major league baseball and touring with Abe Sapperstein in the Midwest and me in the East, he was doing so well that the New York Giants wanted him for the stretch drive. They contacted him and Satch told them, "If you will pay me for the balance of the year what I'm making on this trip, I'll sign up." After Satch told the Giants he was making $15,000 a month, the Giants changed their minds.

If Satch had been in the big leagues in his younger days, he would have been as good as, or better than any pitcher that ever lived. He had absolutely magnificent control, fantastic speed, and a hell of a curve ball. He really didn't need a curve ball because he was so fast and overpowering. He was like Walter Johnson.

Another great star was Josh Gibson. I saw Gibson hit home runs for distances I'd never seen before. I was sitting in the box seat with Clark Griffith, then owner of the Washington Senators, in Griffith Stadium. The Philadelphia Stars played against the Homestead Grays in a double-header. Josh hit three home runs into the left-field stands, which was almost an impossible hit in those days—a 525-foot drive. Very few players hit the ball that far. That year, 1940, in twenty-seven games with the Homestead Grays, Josh hit more home runs in Griffith Stadium than the entire American League, except the Senators, who played all their home games there. If Josh had the opportunity to play in the major leagues, he would have "out-Ruthed" Babe Ruth and Hank Aaron.

Buck Leonard was another outstanding performer. He was as smooth a first baseman as I have ever seen. In those days, the first basemen on the Negro teams took on the roles of clowns or showboats. Each first baseman would have a funny way of catching the ball. But Leonard was strictly baseball. He had a great glove, was a hell of a steady hitter, and drove in a lot of runs. Buck Leonard was just as good as Hal Chase.

Traveling in those days for a black club was tough. When the fellows traveled through the South they couldn't stop anywhere to eat. They either carried sandwiches or looked for a black restaurant. They traveled by bus or automobile. We didn't give them much money to eat because the money just wasn't there. As things got better they got more meal money, and higher salaries, and better conditions. But they had things tough. That's why it is amazing that they could play the kind of baseball they did.

Sometimes a double-header was nothing. When night baseball came in, sometimes we booked triple-headers. They played a double-header in New York against the Bushwicks or somebody, then on the way from New York to Philadelphia they'd stop off and play in some city that had lights, like Trenton, maybe. And they'd play Sundays. On some holidays they'd play three games: morning, noon, and night. It was tough in the early days and they just about survived, but they were doing the thing they liked best. Playing baseball. As most of them used to say, "It beats bell-hopping or mopping floors."

Many of these ballplayers were far superior to many of the whites playing major league ball today. Oscar Charleston, Josh Gibson, Satchel Paige, Cannonball Dick Redding, Joe Rogan, Smokey Joe Williams, and Slim Jones, to name a few. The black leagues had players that would have dominated the majors. Today the black player leads the majors in everything: hitting, fielding, and stolen bases. In 1947, when Jackie Robinson came up, I think he and Campy could have come right up from black baseball instead of playing first in the minors. I think Rickey sent them to the minors to adjust to white ballplayers and white crowds. Since Jackie Robinson's entrance into the majors, the black man has completely dominated the game.

1. Bud Fowler with Keokuk of the Western League in 1885. In 1872 he played second base for a white team in New Castle, Pennsylvania, to become the first black professional ballplayer. *National Baseball Library, Cooperstown, N.Y.*

2. Catcher Moses Fleetwood Walker. In 1884 he became the first black major leaguer when he signed with the Toledo Blue Stockings of the American Association, which at the time was recognized as a major league. *National Baseball Library, Cooperstown, N.Y.*

3. Frank Grant was the fourth black in organized baseball in 1886 behind Bud Fowler, Fleetwood Walker, and George W. Stovey. Grant led his Buffalo Bisons club of the International League in hitting that year, but his teammates refused to sit with him for the team photograph. *National Baseball Library, Cooperstown, N.Y.*

4. Moses Fleetwood Walker's brother, Welday, became the second major league black in July of 1884. Welday's venture into the major leagues was pure luck. Many players of the Toledo Blue Stockings had been badly injured, Moses included, and they needed a ballplayer immediately. Welday turned out to be a more than competent outfielder. *National Baseball Library, Cooperstown, N.Y.*

5. John Donaldson. A left-handed pitcher noted for his grace on the mound and a sharp, breaking curve ball that was faster than most pitcher's fast balls! He reached his peak just before World War I with the All Nations Club, which was made up of men of several races. In 1917, New York Giants manager John McGraw said he would have gladly paid $50,000 for Donaldson's contract if he had been white. *National Baseball Library, Cooperstown, N.Y.*

6. Charlie Grant. In March, 1901, New York Giant manager John H. McGraw tried to sign Grant by passing him off as a Cherokee Indian. He might have gotten away with the ruse if Charles Comiskey, President of the Chicago White Sox, and some of the other owners hadn't seen through the disguise and raised a ruckus. Grant never got to the major leagues and completed his ballplaying career in black baseball. *National Baseball Library, Cooperstown, N.Y.*

7 and 8. John Henry "Pop" Lloyd was a shortstop and coach of the Atlantic City Bacharach Giants from the early 1900s. He is acknoweldged to be one of the greatest baseball players of all time. *National Baseball Library, Cooperstown, N.Y.*

9. Oscar Charleston. From 1915 to 1930, Charleston, a left-handed thrower and batter, who was just under six feet tall, was recognized as the best outfielder in the game. When he grew heavier and lost his speed, he moved to the infield and became a superior first baseman. He was elected to the Baseball Hall of Fame in 1976. *National Baseball Library, Cooperstown, N.Y.*

10. Raliegh "Biz" Mackey, a tremendous hitter, a fierce competitor. He owned a powerful arm, strong enough so that he could throw harder to second base from a squatting position than most catchers could standing up. *National Baseball Library, Cooperstown, N.Y.*

11. Infielder, outfielder Dave Malarcher, Indianapolis ABCs, Detroit Stars, Chicago American Giants (1916-1935). *National Baseball Library, Cooperstown, N.Y.*

12. Bill Yancey. From 1923 to 1936 played as an outstanding shortstop with the Philadelphia Giants, Lincoln Giants, Hilldale Club, New York Black Yankees, Brooklyn Eagles, and the Philadelphia Stars. *National Baseball Library, Cooperstown, N.Y.*

13. Buck Leonard.

14. Buck Leonard, first baseman of the Homestead Grays, who perhaps was a better fielder at his position than Hal Chase or George Sisler; he definitely was a harder hitter than those two.

15. Josh Gibson. "Not only the greatest catcher, but the greatest ballplayer I ever saw," said Roy Campanella. *National Baseball Library, Cooperstown, N.Y.*

16. Josh Gibson.

17 and 18. James Thomas "Cool Papa" Bell. Originally a right-handed batter, Bell taught himself to be a switch-hitter. He was known as the fastest runner who ever played baseball, white or black. *National Baseball Library, Cooperstown, N.Y.*

19. Third baseman William "Judy" Johnson was one of black baseball's most fabulous players. He owned a strong arm and was equally adept at fielding balls to his right and left. *National Baseball Library, Cooperstown, N.Y.*

20. Barnstorming 1955. *Front row (left to right):* Jim Gilliam, Hank Thompson, Willie Mays, Sam Jones, Gene Baker, Ernie Banks, Monte Irvin. *Back row (left to right):* J. B. Martin, owner of the Memphis Red Sox; Don Newcombe, Joe Black, George Crowe, Hank Aaron, Brooks Lawrence, Charley White, Connie Johnson, Larry Doby, Louis Louden. *Monte Irvin.*

21. In my opinion, Red Barber was the greatest baseball announcer that ever lived. I can still hear him bellowing from the radio speaker now: "The Bases are F.O.B. (full of Brooklyns)" or "Dolf Camilli hits a Bedford Avenue Blast (a home run)." Through Barber, I "saw" many a game on the radio.

22. 1946 Washington Grays *(left to right):* Sam Bankhead, SS; Josh Gibson, C; Buck Leonard 1B; Dave Hoskins, RF; Jerry Benjamin, CF. *Walter (Buck) Leonard Collection.*

23. The great Homestead Grays team of 1942 who won the Negro National League pennant by beating out Baltimore Elite Giants. Third from left, second row is Josh Gibson; at far right, standing, is Buck Leonard.

THE
IMPOSSIBLE
DREAM

Jackie Robinson was not a name that I was unfamiliar with: UCLA football, Army baseball and football—he was a total athlete, but I still disregarded the rising myth of the man. I knew that Robinson had been discharged from the Army as lieutenant after three years of service because of bone chips in one of his ankles. I knew that he had joined the Kansas City Monarchs of the Negro National League. I was aware of the man, but I attached no special importance to him. Dumb me! Young me! So unaware of the social changes occurring in America and the courage and defiance of one man: Branch Rickey.

JACKIE ROBINSON

When Jackie Robinson joined the parent Dodger club in 1947 after one year in Montreal, there were at the time sixteen black ballplayers in organized baseball. Fifty percent of them played for the minor league clubs of the Dodgers. The first black in the American League was Larry Doby, the heavy-hitting twenty-two-year-old second sacker of Effa and Abe Manley's

Newark Eagles. In July, infielder Hank Thompson and outfielder Willard Brown of the Kansas City Monarchs were signed by the St. Louis Browns. Both lasted just a few weeks and rejoined the Monarchs. Nineteen forty-seven was the year of portents for the Negro leagues.

With blacks now entering the majors, fan interest in Negro baseball began to wane and attendance began to fall. Most of the black ball clubs began to lose money that year. In 1948 attendance dropped even further. Catcher Roy Campanella joined Jackie Robinson in Brooklyn. Satchel Paige was brought to the Cleveland Indians by Bill Veeck. Satch—at the age of forty-two—had a 6-and-1 record to help Cleveland win the pennant. Paige was "Black Baseball" and his joining of the majors marked the death knell of the Negro leagues.

At the end of 1948 season the powerful Homestead Grays, winners of the Negro National League pennant and the Series, disbanded. When the Newark Eagles and the New York Black Yankees broke up at the end of 1948, the Negro National League ceased operation, ending an uninterrupted sixteen-year run. The clubs left over in the Negro National League joined the Negro American League, which at that time had two divisions. When Sammy Jethroe joined the Boston Braves in 1950 after playing with the Cleveland Buckeyes, only five major league teams had black players: the Dodgers, the Giants, the St. Louis Browns, the Indians, and the Braves. In 1953 seven major league clubs had a total of twenty black ballplayers. In 1957 fourteen clubs had thirty-six players. Total major league integration came in 1959 when the Boston Red Sox added Elijah "Pumpsie" Green to the club.

The clubs in the Negro leagues were not well compensated for their players. The average price ranged between $1,000 and $5,000. During the early years of blacks entering the big leagues, the reported top price paid by the major leagues for a player was $14,000, which the New York Giants supposedly paid the Birmingham Black Barons in 1950 for a young outfielder named Willie Mays. The Dodgers paid that sum for Dan Bankhead in 1949, and the Boston Red Sox coughed up that amount for Piper Davis.

In the early 1950s two of the finest prospects in the Negro American League were Henry Aaron of the Indianapolis Clowns (bought by the Braves in 1952) and Ernie Banks of the Kansas City Monarchs (purchased by the Chicago Cubs in 1953). Pat Scantlebury, pitcher with the New York Cubans, was the last black ballplayer to go directly from a Negro team into the major leagues. He participated in eight games for the Cincinnati Reds in 1956. In 1960 the Negro American League folded, thus ending the great days of Negro baseball.

I will never forget the strange feeling that I had at the Polo Grounds during a championship contest between the Newark Eagles and the Kansas City Monarchs. Jackie Robinson had just enjoyed a successful season with the Montreal Royals in the International League. I remember saying to myself, "To hell with this Black World Series; let's see blacks in the major league fall classic." A year later it happened—Jackie Robinson and the Dodgers vs. the New York Yankees. God damn!

In the twentieth century, big-league baseball saw a lot of changes. The game went from day to night, from coast to coast (before expansion there were only two teams west of the Mississippi: the St. Louis Cardinals and the St. Louis Browns), and then from border to border. By far the most significant change in this century was when the player named Jack Roosevelt Robinson from Cairo, Georgia, opened the 1947 season at first base for the Brooklyn Dodgers of the National League.

In 1873 a Negro infielder named Bud Fowler played with an otherwise all-white team at New Castle, Pennsylvania, and in 1884 a well-educated Negro, Moses "Fleetwood" Walker, caught forty-one games for Toledo at the time the Ohio Metropolis and the American Association were in the major leagues. Four years later, the Negro would disappear from the major leagues for almost the next fifty years. This was somewhat of a backlash of the Civil War's Reconstruction era. Adrian "Cap" Anson, the game's first 3,000-hit player, figured prominently in the prejudice by which an unwritten law, a mislabeled gentleman's agreement, deprived black men of a chance to play in the national pastime. Negro baseball, which former college star and World War II veteran Jackie Robinson turned to in 1945, was largely a disorganized automobile bus tour and junket throughout the country. With the exception of Satch Paige and Josh Gibson, Negro players performed for peanuts.

As a result, Robinson was extremely receptive when he was confronted by Dodger scout Clyde Sukeforth and told that Branch Rickey wanted to talk to him. Robinson believed that Rickey, then the Dodger president, wanted him for his Brooklyn Brown Dodgers, which was in the black Continental League.

The whole Brown Dodgers' affair was a ruse on Rickey's part. He had actually assigned scouts to seek out the best Negro material on hand. Rickey considered the Negro leagues virgin territory and he intended to explore it. Rickey told George McLaughlin, president of the Brooklyn Bank and Trust Company and head of the bank-operated ball club, "We're gonna beat the bushes and take whatever comes out, and that might include a Negro or two."

McLaughlin didn't object and two years later in 1945, two weeks after the war ended, came Rickey's historic confrontation with the twenty-six-year-old Jackie Robinson. Rickey knew all about Robinson: that he was born in Cairo, Georgia on January 31, 1919, and that a year after his father left home his mother, with five children, moved to Pasadena where she did domestic work to feed one and all. Those were hard years. As a matter of fact, many years later when Robinson was a high-salaried player, his wife Rachel had to coax him to eat green vegetables. Jack had grown up on a bread (dunked in sugar and milk) diet.

As the youngest of the Robinson brood, Jack was taken care of by his sister Willie Maye, two years older than Jack, so that Mrs. Robinson could work. Jackie would accompany his sister to school and play in the school yard until she got out of class. The Robinsons lived on Pasadena's Pepper Street, the melting pot of Mexicans, Japanese, and blacks. There was a great deal of juvenile delinquency in the area until a man named Carl Anderson came along and organized sports teams; the trouble then seemed to disappear. Such an impression was made on Robinson that it led to his adult interest in sports. Jack's older brother Mack was a track star who had finished second to Jesse Owens in the 200 meters in the 1936 Olympics in Berlin.

Jack attended Pasadena Junior College and then UCLA, lettering in four sports in both schools. In track he broke the Pacific Coast Conference broad-jump record. In 1941 he played professional football for the Los Angeles Bulldogs. A few months after Pearl Harbor he did basic training in the Army at Fort Riley, Kansas. He was discharged as first lieutenant in November 1944. In 1945 he joined the Kansas City Monarchs at $400 a month.

The complete informality of the Negro leagues used to get on Robinson's nerves. Satch Paige, for example, would pitch two or three innings, travel by private car instead of by bus with the team, and work for various all-star teams the rest of the week. One day in Baltimore, halfway through a game, the official scorer left the ballpark. With this type of lackadaisical setup, Robinson was more than glad to get to New York and sit across from Branch Rickey in Brooklyn that August of 1945, even if it only meant getting into a Negro league with more substance.

At this meeting Rickey startled Robinson by letting him know he wanted to bring him into professional baseball at Montreal, a club that at the time was in the Triple-A International

League, and later maybe, have him join the Dodgers themselves! Rickey, a former attorney, grilled Robinson for three hours in this incredible moment in baseball history. Rickey played the roles of an insulting waiter in a restaurant, a nasty room clerk in a Southern hotel, a sarcastic railway conductor. They went over every possible situation that might arise. "Suppose they throw at your head?" Rickey asked. "Mr. Rickey, they've been throwing at my head for a long time," Robinson replied. "Suppose," Rickey asked, "I am an opposing player in the heat of an important ball game. Suppose I collide with you at second base? When I get up I yell, 'You dirty black bastard!' What do you do then?"

Rickey's executive assistant, former newspaperman Arthur Mann, who witnessed this amazing event, saw Robinson blink, lick his lips, and swallow. "Mr. Rickey," Robinson asked, somewhat puzzled, "do you want a ballplayer who's afraid to fight back?" Rickey shot back with "I want a ballplayer with guts enough *not* to fight back. You've got to do this job with base hits and stolen bases and by fielding ground balls, Jackie, and nothing else! Now I'm playing against you in the World Series, I'm not a hot-headed player, I want to win that game so I go into you spikes first, but you don't give ground. You stand there and you jab the ball in my ribs and the umpire yells 'Out!' I flare up, all I can see is that black face before me, so I punch you in the cheek." Rickey's fist swung through the air and just missed Robinson's face. Robinson's eyes blinked but his head didn't move. Rickey roared at Robinson, "What do you do?" Then Jackie said, "I've got two cheeks, is that it?" This scene over forty-five years ago assured Branch Rickey's success in this "bold" move.

On April 18, 1946, my father and I venture out to Roosevelt Stadium in Jersey City to see the Little Giants of the International League open against the Montreal Royals and Jackie Robinson.

I sat there with tears in my eyes. My mind flashes back to St. Nicholas Avenue, the stickball games, the Polo Grounds, Yankee Stadium, Ebbets Field, my idol Red Barber doing the Dodger games, Mel Allen broadcasting both the Yankees and Giants home games, reading the Sporting News *since I was ten years old, and studying record books where not a single black man was mentioned. Oh God, is it really true? Robinson grounds out his first time up. But before the day is over he has gone 4-for-5, including a home run and two stolen bases, and played second base flawlessly as the Royals win 14–1. Play? He can play. There's no doubt about it. But this is Triple-A. Will they stand for it in the majors? I am still skeptical and so is my father. We never question Jackie's ability, but after so many years we are so brainwashed we just felt the experiment will boomerang in Branch Rickey's face. The very fact that Southerners are in preponderance in the game is enough for me to doubt.*

There was another Negro in the Montreal dugout with Robinson that year: John Wright, a twenty-seven-year-old right-hander who was signed by Montreal following his discharge from the Navy in February, 1946. In the Negro leagues Wright played with the Homestead Grays, the Newark Eagles, and the Pittsburgh Crawfords. Wright, who was with Jackie Robinson during spring training at Sanford, Florida, was optioned to Three Rivers in Quebec in the Class-C border league a month after the season opened. The following winter he was released by the Dodger organization and then he rejoined the Grays. After they optioned John Wright, Roy Partlow, a thirty-year-old Negro pitcher was added to the roster. In June he too was sent to Three Rivers and Robinson finished out the 1946 campaign as the only Negro in the International League, leading the league in hitting with a .349 average. On April 10, 1947, the Dodgers announced the purchase of Robinson's contract from Montreal. He was to report immediately.

Walking up St. Nicholas Avenue between 141st and 145th Streets, looking at the old buildings and garages alongside which we played stickball on the narrow sidewalks. How the hell we did it, I'll never know. From my ninth to my sixteenth birthdays I was the Carl Hubbell, Joe Medwick, Mel Ott, Terry Moore, and Marty Marion of the neighborhood. Sonny Curtis was Red Rolfe, Joe DiMaggio, and Monte Pearson. God, we had the baseball bug! Scrapbooks chock full of autographed baseball pictures. When we didn't attend the games at the Polo Grounds, Yankee Stadium, or Ebbets Field, we would rush upstairs to listen to Red Barber and Mel Allen do the play-by-play. Both of us would rather play ball than eat. What a waste! Blacks would never play major league ball in our lifetime, we thought. I'm glad we were both wrong.

Robinson, who had received a $3,500 bonus and a $600-a-month contract at Montreal, was on his way to the recognition that would bring him up to $42,500 for his contract, plus the share of six World Series and other baseball earnings. Jackie made his reputation as a second baseman and the last four years of his career he played third and the outfield, but he broke in as a first baseman.

Opening day, April 15, 1947. The Dodgers against the Braves at Ebbets Field, with Jackie at first base. Jackie got no hits, but the Dodgers won 5–3 with Jackie scoring the fifth run for Brooklyn. Jackie's first hit in the "bigs" came in the second game of the season off Boston left-hander Glenn Elliot. It was a safe bunt. The first homer came the next day at New York's Polo Grounds off the Giant's Dave Koslo. Robinson's mettle was tested in the Dodgers' first series with the Philadelphia Phillies. Manager Ben Chapman and his players ripped Robinson with racial slurs to the point where he almost dropped his bat and took off for the Philadelphia dugout. But Robinson remembered Rickey's turn-the-other-cheek doctrine and clammed up. The Dodgers' second baseman, Eddie Stanky, was also a great help. The Philadelphia-born Stanky, a resident of Mobile, Alabama, shouted at the Phillies' field leader, "Chapman, why don't you get on somebody who can fight back!" Robinson credited Stanky and the Dodgers' captain, Kentucky-born Pee Wee Reese for support when he needed it.

Robinson was elected Rookie of the Year by the *Sporting News*. He missed only three games, hit .297, and played well around the bag. Robinson hit twelve homers and drove in forty-eight runs.

In 1947 my mother couldn't wait to see Jackie Robinson play so we wandered up to the Polo Grounds one hot July day to see a Giant-Dodger double-header. It was really a weird feeling to see so many blacks in a major league park at one time. My mother laughed and said, "Who's playing today, the Black Yankees and the Homestead Grays?" Man, my people were raising hell in the ballpark that day. I think they would have applauded if Robinson had urinated on home plate. But what the hell, it had been a long time coming. A black ballplayer in the major leagues!

Jackie hit his peak in 1949. He led the league in hitting with a .342 average, beating out Stan Musial of the St. Louis Cardinals in a close race. He had 203 hits, including thirty-eight doubles, twelve triples, sixteen homers, and 124 RBIs. He was named the National League's Most Valuable Player. One of the greatest games Robinson played almost saved the 1951 pennant. The Dodgers had just about wrapped up the race by opening up a thirteen-game lead in mid-August against the Giants. But the Polo Grounders went on a sixteen-game tear and kept on coming, to the point where they actually had the pennant won if the Dodgers lost at Philadelphia. Behind 6–1, the Dodgers tied the game. In the twelfth inning with the bases loaded, Eddie Waitkus hit an apparent game-winning and pennant-deciding line drive to Robinson's right. Jackie made a running back-handed dive at the ball just inches off the ground. He made the catch and when he landed he lay on the ground face down, unconscious. But Jackie shook the cobwebs out of his head and hit a two-run homer in the fourteenth inning to win the game and set up the "Bobby Thomson" playoff with the Giants.

"All major league clubs will have a wary eye cocked on the nation's first baseball school for Negroes run by Negroes when it opens in Greenville, Miss., on February 27th. With the Negroes now an accepted part of the big-league pattern, baseball men realize they must have a source of supply for future players. This school, to be under the direction of Homer Goose Curry of Memphis, is the start in that direction. It will be known as the 'Delta Negro Baseball School.'"
United Press, Memphis, Feb. 11, 1951

Jackie hit and played hard to help win Dodger pennants in 1952 and 1953 and occasionally played third base and outfield to suit the whims of skipper Chuck Dressen. Robinson had his best World Series in 1953, when he hit .320. In 1954, playing third, second, and the outfield, Robbie hit .351.

After all these many years of rooting for the St. Louis Cardinals . . . sitting in the "Jim Crow" right-field pavilion at Sportsman's Park in the 1942 World Series. Idolizing Joe Medwick, Pepper Martin, Stan Musial, Mort Cooper, Terry Moore, Marty Marion, et al., never dreaming blacks would play in the majors, especially in St. Louis, which in those years before expansion and new franchises was the only city that had major league baseball west of the Mississippi. It finally happened, the

Cardinals signed two black players: first baseman Tom Alston and pitcher Brooks Lawrence. That Mayday in 1954 at the Polo Grounds gave me a strange feeling. Never mind Jackie Robinson and the Dodgers in 1947, "niggers" were now playing for "my" Cardinals in the Mound City, the South, Cracker Town, St. Louis, Missouri. Baseball had come full circle for me!

Until the ban was lifted in May of 1944, the covered bleachers of the right field pavilion was the only section in Sportsman's Park where black people were allowed to sit. Talking with Enos "Country" Slaughter on my WABC talk show, I asked him about his awareness or lack of same about the segregated seating in Sportsman's Park when he was playing right field for the St. Louis Cardinals. His response: "I didn't know anything about colored people sitting in the ballpark, but I did notice that all of them sat behind me in right field."

"Top brass of the Hot Springs baseball club scheduled a meeting today, apparently to decide whether they will go through with their controversial plan to use two Negro pitchers. Hot Springs previously offered a compromise to use the Negroes, Jim and Leander Tugerson of Florence Villa, Fla., only at home or in parks where the home team had no objection. George Trautman, president of the National Association of Professional Baseball Leagues, ruled yesterday that the Hot Springs Bathers can play the Negroes in the Cotton States League if they want to and that the Class-C circuit cannot kick the team out."

New York Post, April 16, 1953

When the Dodgers won their first world championship in 1955 in Walter Alston's second season as manager, Robinson hit .256 and played third base and contributed to the World Series victory. Two months after the Dodgers were defeated in the 1956

World Series, on December 13 the Dodgers traded Robinson to the Giants for pitcher Dick Littlefield and $35,000. Robinson announced his retirement from the game, canceling the trade. He was elected to the Hall of Fame in 1962, the first time he was eligible.

"It was a cloudy afternoon in New York's Yankee Stadium and Dave Hoskins, the part-time union auto worker who broke the Texas League's Jim Crow last season, stood in front of the Cleveland Indians dugout and recalled a night at Shreveport, La. 'I got three letters in the same handwriting telling me to stay out,' the slim pitcher recalled. 'One letter said I'd be shot if I as much as sat in the dugout. The second said I'd be shot if I went on the field, even in practice. The third said I would be shot if I went out to pitch the game.'

'What did you do with the letters?' 'Nothing,' he said. 'I knew if I showed them to Dutch Myer, our manager on the Dallas team, he wouldn't let me pitch. Another thing, I didn't want any big fuss, with Shreveport cops all over the place. They'd come around the dugout and all that.'"
New York Daily Worker, April 19, 1953

RACHEL ROBINSON: Jackie and I got married a month before we went to spring training with the Montreal Royals in Vero Beach in 1946. Not only was Jackie entering a new field and was very uncertain about it, but we were going to the South for the first time. The whole experience was compounded by our first entrance into a racially segregated area of the country. We had certainly been through racial discrimination in the North, but in the South it was so blatant we couldn't go into certain places. We were bumped off the first plane and replaced by whites. We had to use segregated facilities and that kind of thing. When we were bumped off the plane, no provisions were made for us to get to Vero Beach for spring training. We had to take a bus and ride in the back of the bus. These were painful things for me, but particularly painful for Jackie because he was such an assertive person and had always been and was very sure of his manhood and so forth. To have seen him kowtow and submit to these indignities was abominable. Despite all the problems, Jackie and I at no time wanted to give up the whole idea of his playing in the majors. We constantly supported one another. We reached the point where we joked about the horrible conditions.

> "Jackie was one of the most exciting ballplayers ever. He didn't impress me at first with his choppy swing, but he proved to be a good hitter, really tough in the clutch. He was a good fielder, too, and a daring, upsetting base-runner. A winner."
>
> *Stan Musial*

> "Sure, there was some grumbling when Jackie came to the League. I guess some of the Southern ballplayers didn't like the idea. But, I tell you, every day that Robinson played he made them eat every word they were saying. He took a lot, but he stuck. I heard him called some awful things by a lot of guys who didn't have the guts to back up what they were saying. Lucky for him, Jackie was playing in the right place. Those Brooklyn fans loved and appreciated him."
>
> *Elbie Fletcher*

When we got to Vero Beach, we were not permitted to live with the team. This we had been warned of by Branch Rickey. I must say that part of the cushion for us was the preparation that Mr. Rickey gave us. I mean he really laid it out for us in terms of what he could see was in store for us. Mr. Rickey scouted out a wonderful family for us to live with near Bethune-Cookman

College. We had heard rumors that certain white players were circulating petitions that they were not going to play with Jackie, that they were going to boycott, or some kind of action. Mr. Rickey kept us clued in to those developments. He would say, "That's what's being planned," and then he would tell us what he planned to do about it—what his strategy was, when they came in to meet with him, he would tell those irate players that they could play for another club. He always indicated that he was ready to back up his experiment. Rickey was quite supportive to us. Nevertheless, Jackie couldn't perform well that first spring because the pressure was so unbearable. He didn't get too many hits until spring training was almost over. He was trying too hard . . . he was overswinging . . . he couldn't sleep at night . . . he had great difficulty concentrating . . . it was rough. I helped Jackie by being with him constantly.

"I don't know anyone who could have stood all the abuse Jackie had to take in breaking into baseball and stuck it out to become the great player he was. When you know the true nature of Jackie . . . what a fighter he was and how he had to keep it inside of him . . . it's just unbelievable. Thinking back on it, I'm just glad I got to play alongside Jackie and be a part of history."
Pee Wee Reese

I went everywhere with him. We got up together in the morning, we had breakfast together, and I went to the ballpark with him. We didn't socialize at all. We stayed isolated to some extent . . . that was one of the ways we sort of maintained ourselves. Jackie felt the pressure of the black people who were counting on him. Those first years of exhibition games just drew, drew, drew huge crowds. Take a place like West Palm Beach, where they drew a larger black crowd than white and yet they had a very small segment of the stands set aside for blacks. It was just outrageous. It became so that they came through a hole in the fence and not through the turnstile. They literally took boards out of the fence.

The black fans were so eager to come in and so excited about what was happening that they just kept pouring in. It was like seeing cattle coming through that hole in the fence. We knew that the ball clubs were profiting from their presence, yet they would not give them decent accommodations. I finally got so I couldn't go into the ballpark. I would sit in the car. I just couldn't stand to see my people treated like animals. The fly balls would come out into the middle of the crowd and they would scatter to let the players get in there to get the ball.

When we got to Montreal in 1946 the fans there did not seem to have the same racial hangups that we had experienced all through the South. We found a more favorable environment. We lived in a French Canadian neighborhood where people didn't even speak English and we were kind of curiosities. When they finally found out who we were it was beautiful.

Jackie's first manager in Montreal, Clay Hopper, never really believed in this but he was just doing as he was told. I thought he just saw Jackie as a commodity. He just evaluated Jackie as somebody who could help him win, somebody who drew crowds, somebody who could spark up the games and most of all, somebody who Mr. Rickey was intent on holding. Therefore it was Hopper's job to make it work. In other words, Hopper knew he was stuck with Jackie. Hopper never went out of his way to be abusive and he never went out of his way to be friendly. As he chewed on his tobacco, he said Jackie was doing his job. Hopper was a Mississippian. He played Jackie only as much as he had to play him. At the end of the season, Clay appeared to come around to some extent, but you could never distinguish between whether he was feeling that Jackie was more of a human and he had learned something in this experiment or whether he was just happy to have a winning ball club.

Branch Rickey looked upon Jackie as a human being. I can vouch for that fact. Of course I realize Branch was a shrewd businessman. I'm sure he saw Jackie as a good business move. On the other hand, there were times he could have dropped the whole thing. Or he could have said, "I tried but it didn't work out." There were so many ways he could have done that.

On the Dodgers, Carl Furillo, Dixie Walker, and Kirby Higbe didn't go for Jackie at all. Pee Wee Reese initially looked at Jackie as someone competing for his job, but later he and Jackie teamed up . . . when he saw they could work together. Carl Erskine was strongly in Jackie's corner from the start. Given the fact that the Dodgers began to win, like Montreal did the year before, people tended to forget the racial problems. Winning the pennant and getting to the World Series and becoming a championship team was the utmost. Those thoughts took over.

Jackie never let things slide by him; that is, he never let anyone get away with any slighting remarks without taking them up. He would not let them forget that he was not able to have all the privileges they had. A funny thing—in that first year when Jackie was ridden unmercifully by the opposition—racial epithets, and whatnot, it got so vicious that even those Dodgers who were opposed to Jackie at the club started to rally to his defense. The most vicious attacks on Jackie came from Ben Chapman and the rest of the Philadelphia Phillies. Chapman claimed his bench jockeying was in the tradition. His attacks were personal and abusive, way outside the tradition.

In the winter of 1947 Jackie said, "Okay, I've taken all the abuse and indignities, but now I've earned my place. I've demonstrated my talents, abilities, and competence. I'm going to let loose in 1948." This was Jackie's plan whether Mr. Rickey approved or not. This was a turning point for Jackie because, as is always the case, so many liberal whites will help someone get started and want to maintain control over their behavior. The minute blacks want to become independent and do their own thing their own way, they are either dumped or told they're going too fast. But Mr. Rickey went along all the way with Jackie.

Contrary to the general feeling, Jackie was not a bitter man. Jackie was the kind of person who when he saw things going wrong just couldn't let it happen. He had to say what he felt, even under the threat of being hurt himself. Jackie was a deeply religious person. He had a striking humility. He felt he had an obligation to do things for his people and for his family. He felt he had been chosen somehow to be the first black in the major leagues . . . that this was some kind of mission for him. He intended to carry it out at all costs.

Jackie Robinson died October 24, 1972, in New York.

LARRY DOBY

LARRY DOBY: I can't say what motivated me to play baseball despite my knowing black men were not playing in the majors. I guess you have to talk about the situation of the late Jackie Robinson. During that time Mr. Rickey decided that he wanted to have a black ballplayer and signed Jackie for his Montreal baseball club. I think every black youngster who was interested in baseball at that time, and we're talking about 1945 and 1946,

"Most of Doby's experience in baseball had been at shortstop and second base. But there was little room at those positions on the Indians, what with manager-player Lou Boudreau at short and Joe Gordon, whom the clubs had purchased from the Yankees that winter, playing second. But Doby had the stuff; he was moved to the outfield and he became a superstar."

Bill Veeck

must have thought about playing major league baseball. You had a person to identify with, and whenever you went out to the streets to play stickball or baseball, you were playing like Jackie Robinson. I think that motivated me.

"Ninety-four-and-a-half years after Abe Lincoln delivered his Emancipation Proclamation, baseball the other day witnessed a complete emancipation of the American Negro in America's traditional game. Larry Doby, a colored player of the Chicago White Sox, dared to take a punch at Art Ditmar, a white pitcher of the Yankees, and history was made. Never before in the eleven years since the bars were dropped and colored players admitted, albeit gingerly, to the major leagues, had a Negro thrown the first punch in a player argument. There is no intent to condone what Doby did, but merely to point out that the consequences fell far short of civil war, or a secession, or a violent sense of outrage except among Ditmar's Yankee teammates who dashed to his assistance, but in no more anger than if his attacker had been a white player. Now this was no white pitcher dusting off a Negro batter simply because of pigmentation, but the Doby-Ditmar episode had special significance because for the first time a Negro player was daring to get as assertive as a white man whose special province organized ball had been for nearly a hundred years."

Shirley Povich, June 13, 1957 at Comiskey Park
Sporting News, 1957

I was in the service at the time Jackie got signed. I was on a little island in the Pacific. There were a couple of major league players on the island at the time also, fellows by the name of Mickey Vernon of the Washington Senators and Billy Goodman of the Boston Red Sox, and of course during that time we would go out with each other and have batting practice, pitching to each other. They mentioned quite often that if blacks got the opportunity that I should have the opportunity to be a baseball player. I think that was the first time I thought about being in baseball.

If you ask me about my earlier life in high-school baseball, there was nobody for me to identify with. Unless you identified yourself with Joe DiMaggio if you played center field, Joe Gordon if you played second base, or Frank Crosetti if you played shortstop. This was a little odd, because you couldn't say, "I'm going to be a major league ballplayer like these people," because there were no black players involved. What we did in our neighborhood was become these people. It was kind of a fantasy because you never thought black people would ever play baseball in the major leagues. But when Jackie got involved it gave me some identification. Then I wanted to play major league ball. Jackie played many positions: first, second, third, and the outfield. There were a lot of positions where a black man could identify with Jackie. Frankly, at first my thing was football. There I could identify with blacks like Buddy Young, Marion Motley, and Ozzie Simmons. I used to listen to Ohio State games broadcast by Bill Stern and I said to myself, "I'd like to hear him call my name one of those days." Blacks were playing and that's what I wanted to get involved in.

Truthfully, playing baseball back then with the Newark Eagles was fun; I enjoyed it. Of course, back then it was called Negro baseball. You talk about the ghetto, you talk about most blacks being born in the ghetto but enjoying life nonetheless. In the same way, if you played Negro baseball, you played it because you enjoyed doing it.

I was first approached by the Cleveland outfit around June, 1946. Bill Veeck sent a fellow by the name of Louis Jones around to talk to me. He was Veeck's public-relations man at the time. He told me the Indians were interested in me. They had already spoken to Mr. Abe Manley, who along with his wife Effa owned the Eagles. But I didn't know much about it and finally I said I'd be interested in playing. They asked me if I thought I could play major league ball. I was then a kid of twenty-one but I knew I could play in any league, white or black. I was outstanding in the Negro leagues and I knew I could be the same in the majors. A little before this, a fellow named Al Campanis told Roy Campanella that the Dodgers were interested in me.

Roy called me and told me that in about a week or so I'd probably be in Montreal. This was in the spring of 1947. By this time Bill Veeck had gotten in touch with Branch Rickey and it was then decided that I would be the black player representing the American League, since Jackie was representing the National League. With Jackie already there, this was the reason, I guess, I didn't get to the Dodgers.

I'll never forget my first day with the Indians. I made my debut as a pinch hitter for Bryan Stephens, a pitcher, in the seventh inning of a game against the White Sox at Chicago, July 5th. I was struck out by Earl Harris. The following day I played a full game for the Indians at first base, replacing Eddie Robinson, and made one scratch hit in five tries. I wasn't really scared; the toughest part for me was being able to communicate with newspapermen. You were dealing with about twenty or so newspaper people, and some of the questions you answered came out a little differently in the papers.

Any time you're involved in pioneering in any field and being black, you have the problems any black would have. Just like Jackie had in Montreal, I had mine in Cleveland. Because I went straight from Newark to Cleveland there were many people who resented my being on the club, some because I was black, some because they thought I would take their job. But there was the Cleveland pitcher, Mel Harder. He was the guy that was always nice to me.

In 1938 I vividly remember an incident that occurred outside the Polo Grounds on Eighth Avenue after a Giant-Cleveland Indian exhibition game. Mel Harder, the Indian right-hander, hugged and greeted a black friend of his outside the visiting team's clubhouse door. My impressions were varied. I said, Hell, if he can hug the black guy outside, then why can't they play inside together? Maybe there's hope. I approached Harder for an autograph, and as he signed his name I asked if he thought Negro players would ever play in the major leagues. He gave me a positive yes answer. When I got home I told my father what Harder had said. Dad laughed and said, "He was only being nice to you. It will never happen."

But some of them gave me a rough time. I don't want to mention any names. When I walked into the clubhouse in Chicago all the players were lined up against their lockers. Manager Lou Boudreau started introducing me right down the line. For example, he'd say, "Larry Doby, this is Joe Gordon." And each would shake my hand. Out of the twenty-four players I was introduced to, about ten of them didn't put their hands out. The next year Bill Veeck eliminated about five of the guys who were discourteous to me.

You know, Bill Veeck was just as important to me as Branch Rickey was to Jackie Robinson. Veeck told me to curb my temper and to turn the other cheek. The guy really motivated me. There were places my wife, my daughter, and I couldn't go into. Veeck would say, "If they can't go in, I won't go in." Veeck was quite a man, a great man. I think of him as my second father.

At the beginning, I was told by some of the American League players and some of the people in the stands that I was playing in the wrong league, that I was supposed to be in the National League, where the other black son of a bitch was. Despite all this, I had a lot of great thrills in the majors. One of my biggest was concerned with spring training when both the Indians and the Giants were training in Arizona. Cleveland was in Tucson and New York was in Phoenix. After breaking camp we'd play through the South up to the North. In my first full year, the spring of 1948, we were playing a game in Houston. My first time up I got a lot of boos from the fans, who were predominantly white. I hit a home run over the center field fence and was told that only one other person had ever done that and that was Jimmy Foxx. The next time I came up the stands were quiet and then I felt kind of good.

The next big thing that happened to me was also in 1948. We won the pennant and that was the first Indian flag since 1920. I hit a home run off Boston right-hander Johnny Sain in the fourth game of the World Series. We won the game 2–1. Steve Gromek was the winning pitcher and we were hugging each other. This picture appeared on the front pages of papers across the country. This was the first time there were black and white ballplayers embracing in a picture. That was a thrill for me. In the 1954 World Series against the Giants, Willie Mays's fantastic grab off the bat of Vic Wertz was one of the greatest catches I've ever seen. That's got to be one of my greatest thrills. Playing against those great Yankee ball clubs and being a part of the great competition made me feel good. Being able to hit a ball into the center field bleachers at Yankee Stadium, where only two other guys, Babe Ruth and Mickey Mantle, had ever hit, was a thrill. Then there were those tape-measure shots I hit at Griffith Stadium. Those home runs really turned me on.

When I arrived in Cleveland Jackie Robinson called me. The first thing we discussed was the hotel and food situation. These were the two most important things. After you play a hard game of ball and you want to sit down and eat and you have your family with you and you can't, it really bothers you. We put up with this in the Negro leagues, but now that we were major leaguers we wanted the same treatment as the white players. This bugged us more than anything else.

Blacks have had a tremendous effect on the major leagues. People used to think the black player was dumb and played baseball on reflex and instinct. Now they see that the black ballplayer has intelligence. I feel that baseball is far behind in hiring managers and coaches and front-office people that are black. Baseball people feel a black man can't handle people properly. Hell, you don't have to have a degree in psychology to handle people. Psychology has been part of the black man for a long time.

EMMETT L. ASHFORD
THE FIRST BLACK UMPIRE IN MAJOR LEAGUE
BASEBALL

EMMETT ASHFORD: I started umpiring one day in 1937 in a Los Angeles sandlot when the regular umpire didn't show up. Pandemonium ensued, but I received a nice sum of money after the collection was taken up around the park. I didn't then think of umpiring as a career, but when I got out of the Navy in Corpus Christi, Texas, in 1947, a little after Jackie Robinson was signed, I began to think about it seriously.

I came out of the Navy, got back to Los Angeles and got involved as an official in the school-system baseball setup. I was a success. Then I officiated basketball and football games and I began to work for USC and UCLA and the college circuit. I decided the only thing left to do was to get into pro ball. There had been some professional scouts from the majors following me around when I was umpiring in college and they arranged a tryout for me. This was in 1951. The tryout was outside the continental limits because, I guess, they didn't want any kind of explosion. So they arranged for it in Mexicali, Mexico, right across from El Centro, where the temperature ran about 115 in the day and 110 at night.

I was supposed to work a four-game series on the July Fourth weekend. I dashed down to Mexicali and I told the guard at the border, "Me umpire." So one of them reached down and picked up a broken beer bottle and said, "You umpire? The last umpire leave here pretty quick!" I went to the ballpark anyway. At the park another crisis ensued—the white umpires refused to work with me! They had a full house, but the game was held up and they played Latin music over the P.A. system to entertain the fans while they tried to get somebody to come out and work the bases for me. Finally I worked the entire four-game series between Mexicali and Tucson—behind the plate. The fans ate up my performance. When you please the fans in Latin America, you've got it made!

A week later the president of the league called me and asked me if I wanted to finish the season out. So I rushed to the Postmaster's Office, where I was working at the time, and got a leave of absence and finished up the season, plus working for the playoffs. The following year they sent me a contract for the full season (1952), but the Postmaster was under fire then and I couldn't get a leave of absence. So at that point, I resigned with fifteen years' seniority in the Post Office to go out and gamble on baseball.

As luck would have it, after I got out there, about mid-season I get a call from the president of the league (in Los Angeles) saying the league had folded, telling me to come back. So you know how I felt about then. We had six umpires in the league and in those days we had fifty-seven minor leagues, so there was no problem for them to place the five other white umpires, but me being new and black presented a problem. So I took off and went to Ensenada and lay out on the sand. I took a look at the water and thought about going in and not coming out—I was really ready to commit suicide. It was that serious.

Anyway, two days later I got a call about a job in El Paso, Texas (Class C). The league had regrouped and they had reformed, but it was still called the Arizona-Texas League. I went into El Paso unheralded and unsung. They didn't know I was coming. So by the time I got to the park there were two policemen. By the third inning there were fifteen policemen. I was supposed to be replacing an umpire who was retiring because of poor health and this guy stuck me behind home plate. I ran into a grudge series between Chihuahua and El Paso. I think my first call was on Barney Sorrell of El Paso at third base. Then I heard a raucous voice saying, "Nigger, why don't you go back to California! I don't want you out there trying to do a white man's job!" I looked up at him and said, "If you go home and put on some shoes, maybe then we can discuss the matter!"

About the fifth inning the score was tied and Chihuahua had Marvin Williams, one hell of a black hitter. He was the home-run terror of the league, and he came up with two men on, the score tied, and two outs. The trick, of course, was to get him out any way they could. The count was 2-and-2. I called a pitch a ball and the pitcher, catcher, and the manager who was playing second base ganged up on me—I felt like General Custer. They had a real council of war going. I told them then, "I know where I am and I know what the score is but if I have to go out of here with my boots on, that's the way it's going to be." I added, "Look, I'm going over to get some baseballs, and if by the time I come back, you guys are not back at your positions, there will be a forfeit." It worked and I think El Paso went on to win it 6–5 that night. But the most promising thing the next morning was the *El Paso Press*. They called my stand a great display of guts and courage, plus damn good umpiring.

In 1953 I went up to the Western International League, which in those days stretched from Victoria to Vancouver, B.C., over to Edmonton and Calgary. It was a ten-team league in those days (Class-A). I went up there, and then in 1954 the Pacific Coast League brought me in. I stayed there for twelve years. The last three years I was the *Umpire-in-Chief*.

In 1966, my first season in the majors, I was scheduled to work the presidential opening in Washington, D.C., with the Senators and the Yankees. The media really ganged up on me in my hotel room. It was like Grand Central Station. I went out to the park in a cab—the Secret Service was all around the place—Vice-President Hubert Humphrey was to throw out the first ball. The first stop was at the parking lot and the cab driver told a Secret Service man, "I've got one of the umpires here," and the Secret Service man said, "Who are you kidding?" Then the Secret Service man started thumbing through a folder he had with a list of names, still keeping an eye on me, perhaps trying to remember if he had seen me on the Post Office walls. Finally he came to the last page and said, "What's that name again?" I told him and he looked at me in utter disbelief. Then he let us in. You know, that scene was repeated twice more before I got to the umpire's room. But after I got dressed and went out on that field and saw that full stadium, there was a lump in my throat. Then I knew all those years of perseverance and labor were well worth it.

The roughest time in the leagues and I'd rather not say names, were given to me by two or three players and one or two managers who were just not ready for a black umpire. But I had to go ahead and do the job. The reception from the fans and the players was very good. As far as the reception from my fellow umpires, that was a little rough because coming into the majors I was getting ready to work with a bunch of guys who hadn't been close to a black man before, and the only versions they knew about us were what they read in the books and saw in the movies. With my education and background, I guess it was a little rough for some of them.

Overall, any umpire coming into the majors in those days had to go through some sort of initiation process because it was kind of a club up there. I got my share and a little more, but thank heavens for my background that I was able to withstand it and go on and do a creditable job.

I think the average black who says he wants to go into baseball as an umpire doesn't realize what it takes to be an umpire. It takes 1) unimpeachable integrity, 2) perseverance on the job, and 3) dedication to want to do it. The trademarks of any good umpire. It used to take sacrifices, but nowadays we have the umpiring schools, which a lot of blacks are now attending. When I hit the majors in 1966, the black guys started attending umpire school. Most of the blacks who go to these schools think you can attend the school and then jump right into the majors. That's all they know. They look at TV and see the umpire standing out there and think it's an easy job. There is no way you can make an umpire overnight. Once you get out of umpiring school, if you have anything, it will take at least five years to get to the majors.

Emmett Ashford died on March 1, 1980. Today there are only two black umpires in the major leagues: Eric Gregg and Charlie Williams, both of the National League.

THE MORNING STARS

WILLIE MAYS

"Willie ranks with DiMaggio as the best I ever saw. He's a perfect ballplayer, too. Mays can beat a club with his bat, his glove, his arm, and his legs. Look at it either way you'd like: he's stolen more bases than any other home-run hitter who ever lived and hit more homers than any base stealer, past or present. The guy plays with a contagious enthusiasm. Why, he can run better and faster, looking back over his shoulder to see where the ball is, than most players can digging for the next base with head down."

Stan Musial

"I wouldn't trade Willie even up for anybody in baseball."

Leo Durocher

In 1950 the Giants were desperate. They badly needed a first baseman to play with one of their Class-A farm clubs. They received information that just the guy to fill their needs was with the Birmingham Black Barons. However, once the two Giant scouts arrived at the ballpark they forgot all about the first baseman. They saw Willie Mays play center field. Before the game was over, they were on the phone to New York. "This is the greatest player we've ever seen," they told Jack Schwarz, secretary of the Giants' farm system, over the long-distance hookup. "We're afraid to let this go until morning. How high can we go for him?" Almost before the phones were hung up, the Giants purchased Willie's contract from the Barons.

It was perfectly fitting for Number 24 to say good-by with the New York Mets in New York in 1973. For twenty-two years he had given it all: on the base paths, in the outfield, and from the plate. It was time that Willie Mays said good-by to baseball, and he said it standing on home plate. And now it was time that the fans said "Say Hey" to him.

It all started in 1950 because of what Giant scout Eddie Montague thought of a nineteen-year-old outfielder with the Birmingham Black Barons. The Giants gave Birmingham $14,000 for Mays and assigned him to Trenton, a Class-B team. Mays had much success with Trenton in his first professional season. He hit .353 and was rewarded the following season with a ticket to Minneapolis. In his first thirty-five games, Mays hit an astounding .477. Next stop: New York.

The Giants under Leo Durocher were out to beat the Dodgers. They needed the strong hitting of a Willie Mays. But in his first twelve official at-bats, Mays had no hits and six strike-outs. He finally went to Durocher in desperation and asked to be taken out of the lineup. Durocher responded, "You're my center fielder, even if you don't get a hit the rest of the season." By season's end, Willie had hit twenty home runs and knocked in sixty-eight runs. The Giants, much like Willie, made one of the most remarkable comebacks in baseball history that season. They had trailed league-leading Brooklyn by thirteen and a half games during August. But the Giants caught and tied the Dodgers on the last day of the season and beat them in a three-game playoff climaxed by Bobby Thomson's home run in the bottom of the ninth inning of the final game. The pennant came to New

York and Willie won the National League's award for Rookie of the Year.

In 1952, after appearing in only thirty-four games, Mays went into military service. He returned in 1954 and began to tear up the league. In 151 games Willie batted .345 with 195 hits, forty-one home runs, and 110 RBIs. The Giants again won the pennant. In the World Series against the American League champion Cleveland Indians, Willie made an unbelievable catch of a drive off the bat of Vic Wertz. Willie raced to deep center field, approximately 460 feet away from home plate, stuck up his glove, and made the catch that people still talk about today. The Giants won the series in four games. Mays had an electrifying quality that inspired his club, an intangible effect that cannot be reflected in batting averages or fielding records.

The Giants, when he joined them in May of 1951, were in sixth place; his contribution to the miracle of Coogan's Bluff was a substantial one. He played with a rare élan, many times losing his cap during mad dashes on the bases. He ranged far and wide to convert impossible catches into routine plays. Durocher, who sometimes spoke rather harshly to players for whom he had less regard, understood him perfectly, nursed him carefully, and let him play his own game. Mays had fine instincts and could remember signs, but he could not readily recall all the names of persons, so he would start every conversation with "Say hey," the phrase that became his trademark.

The Giants left New York after the 1957 season as Horace Stoneham moved west to San Francisco. Willie followed. Along the trail between 1951 and 1973, Willie established himself as a future occupant in the Hall of Fame. He led the league in home runs four times, hitting his season high of fifty-two in 1965. He is third in career home runs with 660, third only to Hank Aaron and Babe Ruth. He batted over .300 ten different seasons.

He was named the National League's Most Valuable Player in 1954. He was named to the National League's All-Star team every season from 1954 to 1973. He has hit four home runs in one game, tying the major league record. It was fitting that Willie should end his career in New York. He joined the New York Mets in May 1972 in a trade that sent Charlie Williams to the Giants along with $50,000. Moreover, the Mets contract with him gave Mays lifetime security. Mays made an auspicious debut with the Mets against his former teammates on May 14. With the score tied 4–4, Mays sent a long drive over the wall in left center field to win the game for the Mets.

Willie Mays announced his retirement to a packed house at Shea Stadium in New York in September of 1973. With tears in his eyes, he looked up at the crowd which had gathered to honor him and said, "Willie, say good-by to America."

WILLIE MAYS (on his famous catch off Vic Wertz in the 1954 World Series): Wertz hit the ball a long way. But it was to straightaway center in the Polo Grounds . . . and you could hit them a long way to straight center at the Polo Grounds. I turned my back and ran, looked over my shoulder once to gauge the flight of the ball, then kept running. I caught it over my shoulder . . . spun and threw . . . and Davey Williams had come out to take the relay, and on the sequence Doby managed to tag and go to third, while Rosen didn't go anywhere. I think the throw was the remarkable thing, because the ball did get back there in a hurry, and I was a good 450 feet out when I caught it. The catch wasn't all that difficult. Any ball you go a long way for is exciting to the fans in the stands. They're not looking at you when you get the jump on it . . . at that moment, they're looking at the hitter. I'd gotten the good jump . . . had plenty of running room, and the ball stayed up for me.

I was with the Giants for twenty years, and if you would watch them and the way they played, you would see we would play sometimes seven or eight blacks on the field at the same time. To me, when you do that you have a lot of nerve to put that together. I remember one time in Atlanta... we played nine black guys. When you do that in the South you have to have a lot of nerve.

Stoneham did something else too . . . the case of Hank Thompson, the Giants' best player in the 1954 World Series. Even though me and Dusty Rhodes got all the headlines, it was Thompson who made that series move more than anybody else. After his career with the Giants was over, Thompson got into a lot of non-baseball trouble. Horace Stoneham helped him get clear of it. Thompson broke into the majors with the St. Louis Browns along with Willard Brown in 1947.

I don't know the motives of the Browns . . . what with St. Louis being a Southern city with separate rest rooms for white and black in the train station and the hotels were all segregated. St. Louis, however, had a good-size black population. And since the Browns were not drawing white fans, somebody told me they got the idea they could attract black business by bringing in black players. Thompson didn't make it with them, lasting only twenty-five games. But two years later Stoneham brought him up. Here was a black boy who had "failed" but was being given a second chance. The Giants were the first team to my knowledge that went in for bringing a black boy up, then sending him down, then bring him up again. This to me was complete racial equality in baseball. Before Stoneham, a black player would have only one chance to fail. White boys had many.

I almost became a Brooklyn Dodger. I was playing in Birmingham at the time and Artie Wilson was the shortstop and also served as a sort of a Dodger Scout, too. He was coming to Oakland at the time. Chuck Dressen was the manager there, and Wilson told me that next year he would try to take me to spring training in California with Chuck and Oakland. Oakland was a Dodger farm club at the time. Wilson called Chuck and told him, "We have scouted Mays and we don't feel he can hit the breaking ball right now, so we can't use him." A few months later the Giants scouted me and I was signed immediately.

When I started with Trenton, New Jersey, in the Interstate League in 1950, I played there for three months. That was something like Jackie Robinson breaking into the majors. I was there by myself. It was a strange experience for me because I had to really stay apart from the ballplayers. When I say apart, I mean they would drop me off at different hotels, then at game time they would pick me up. But I wanted to play so bad that those kinds of things didn't worry me. I felt that if I could survive that kind of treatment, I thought I could come to the majors very quickly.

Horace Stoneham to me was just as important to the black ballplayer as Branch Rickey. He didn't have a racial barrier. He was a man who, if you could play baseball, you could play on the Giants when I was there. He proved that over the years by having so many black players.

When I joined the Giants, Hank Thompson and Monte Irvin were just like fathers to me. They took good care of me; they saw to it that I was in bed by ten or eleven o'clock at night. I admired both of them. I knew by coming to New York at an early age, if I didn't have advice from those fellows, I couldn't have made it.

SATCHEL PAIGE

"Satchel was the fastest pitcher I ever saw . . . I don't know anybody who had a ball any faster than Satchel. For a long time Satchel just had a fast ball . . . didn't have a curve ball . . . but he finally developed a curve ball, and then he was much rougher."
Buck Leonard

1. Avoid fried meats, which angry up the blood.
2. If your stomach disputes you, lie down and pacify it with your cool thoughts.
3. Keep the juices flowing by jingling around gently as you move.
4. Go very light on the vices, such as carrying on in society. The social ramble ain't restful.
5. Avoid running at all times.
6. Don't look back. Something might be gaining on you.

Words of wisdom by Satch

LeRoy "Satchel" Paige *was* Negro baseball in the nineteen thirties and early forties. Paige was the majordomo in black baseball. He was the Babe Ruth of the black leagues, in the sense that he had that charisma, that certain something which made the turnstiles spin. Black baseball owed a great debt to Paige. In many instances he was "the franchise" for some of the Negro clubs.

How great was Satchel Paige? One of those who knew him was Dizzy Dean. "I know who's the best pitcher I ever saw, and it's old Satchel Paige, that big lanky colored boy." Dean once lost an exhibition heart-breaker to Paige, who beat Dean 1–0 in seventeen innings after Dizzy's great 30–7 year in 1934, plus his two victories over the Detroit Tigers in the World Series. It was the Paige All-Stars vs. Diz Dean All-Stars. Rogers Hornsby knew because Paige struck him out five times one day; Charles Gehringer and Jimmy Foxx knew because Paige struck them out three times each in one game.

Paige would tour the country pitching at times for a team and at other times for himself. His solo performances were billed as "Satchel Paige, World's Greatest Pitcher, Guaranteed to

Strike Out the First Nine Men." He did that more often than not. Paige would then pick up his money and move on to the next town for the next exhibition. With the Pittsburgh Crawfords for three years, and with Josh Gibson as his battery mate, records indicate that Paige won about 110 games.

Of his days of full flower, Satchel Paige says: "I throwed nothing but bee balls and trouble balls then. They batted by ear. They couldn't see me. The world knew about my fast ball. But the best ones were my looper, nothing ball, bat dodger, and hurry-up ball." His "hesitation pitch" was banned by the then American League President Will Harridge as "deceitful." Paige says, "I ain't never throwed an illegal pitch. . . . Just once in a while I used to toss one that ain't never been seen by this generation."

Paige was born in Mobile, Alabama, on July 7, 1906. In 1924 Satchel pitched for the Mobile Tigers, a black semi-pro team. After playing for several semi-pro clubs in the Mobile area during the next two years, he joined the Chattanooga Black Lookouts in 1926 for $50 a month. In 1928 he was sold to the Negro National League's Birmingham Black Barons, where he was given a contract for $275 a month. Paige stayed with the Barons until 1930. However, the club was doing so poorly in attendance that in 1931 Paige was sold by the Barons to the Nashville Elite Giants. That same year the Elite Giants were transferred to Cleveland, where they played all their games in a small ballpark just outside the Cleveland Indians' stadium before the club broke up.

Gus Greenlee, a Pittsburgh numbers operator, was then forming the Pittsburgh Crawfords. He signed Satchel Paige for $250 a month. From 1931 through 1938, Paige was the mainstay of the Crawfords' staff. During the summer of 1938 Paige pitched the summer season in the Mexican league. There he developed a sore arm and upon returning to the United States, a doctor told him he would never pitch again. His arm was so sore he couldn't lift it above his head. At thirty-two years of age, it looked as if Paige's career was at an end.

Early in 1939, Paige was offered employment as a pitcher and first baseman for the Kansas City Monarchs' second team. The Monarchs were a team that barnstormed through the Northwest and into Canada all year around. The Monarchs' owners were still behind Paige because he was good box office even if he didn't pitch well. During that period, with a team billed as the Satchel Paige All-Stars, Paige hurled in small town after small town, painfully pushing his pitches up to the plate then. But one day he got it back; the arm pains subsided and his "bee ball" returned. Immediately Paige was recalled by the Kansas City Monarchs' first team. He stayed with the club successfully until 1948, when he joined the Cleveland Indians.

The Indians were making a run for the flag and needed some pitching insurance. On July 9, 1948, two days after his forty-second birthday, Satchel Paige became the first Negro to hurl in the American League.

Nineteen forty-eight. Cleveland Indians and Yankees at the Stadium. Satchel Paige is hurling for the "Tribe." I can't believe that just ten years ago I was sitting in this same park and witnessed a Negro National League game with Paige, Josh Gibson, and Roy Campanella. Black ballplayers in the "bigs." Unbelievable!

Satchel Paige made a two-inning relief appearance against the St. Louis Browns in Cleveland. In that game Paige gave up two hits and no runs in two innings. Pitching in twenty-one games, Paige won six and lost one as Cleveland won the flag in one hell of a race that wound up in a playoff game against Boston. They went on to win the World Series, beating the Boston Braves in six games. Satch was in the fall classic for only one inning. In 1949 Paige was with the Indians again, winning four and losing seven. He was let go at the end of that season, and he started barnstorming again.

"If some major league club owner had signed Satchel Paige in 1934, the Negro hurler would have gone down in history as the greatest pitcher of all time." That was the opinion of Ray L. Doan, veteran Davenport, Iowa, promoter, under whose auspices Paige had appeared in many barnstorming games. While Doan never acted as Paige's manager, he often arranged for the use of Satchel's services through Gus Greenlee, owner of the Pittsburgh Crawfords, and T. Y. Baird of the Kansas City Monarchs, the two clubs he was with from 1931 to 1948. After the 1934 World Series the promoter arranged a barnstorming tour featuring Dizzy and Paul Dean, supported by a cast of major and the top minor league players.

In a game in Cleveland the Dean All-Stars faced a team of Black All-Stars with Paige on the mound. Satchel pitched the first six innings against Doan's major and minor leaguers and struck out sixteen of the first eighteen men to face him. Not a batter was even able to reach first base. The following day in Columbus, Ohio, Paige pitched the first three innings. "He fooled around as he liked to do," related Doan. "He deliberately walked the first three batters, then he struck out Mickey Heath, Danny Taylor, and Nick Cullop in succession."

In the same year, 1934, Doan entered a House of David team in the semi-pro tournament at Denver, Colorado. He acquired Paige's services especially for the tournament. As expected, Satch pitched and easily won two games. "Satch was supposed to pitch the seventh game," said Doan. "However, he did it in typical Paige fashion, clowning before the game, such as warming up while kneeling. Grover Alexander, who was managing the club for me gave Satch a dressing-down and he quit." Doan used to say that his only difficulty with Paige was in making sure he would always appear at the time and place he was scheduled.

From 1951–53 Paige played with the St. Louis Browns under Bill Veeck, who was the president of the club. His 1953 stint was his last full season in the major leagues. (Paige did make a three-inning appearance with the Kansas City A's in 1965.) He went back to the Negro leagues after his release by the Browns. In 1956 Bill Veeck hired him again to pitch for Miami in the International League. He remained there through 1958. In 1961 he had a brief fling with the Portland Beavers in the Pacific Coast League.

Satchel Paige was elected to the Baseball Hall of Fame in 1971. He died on June 8, 1982, in Kansas City, Missouri.

There was an A&P store on 141st and Edgecomb Avenue where we did our grocery shopping. I remember having my mother buy all those boxes of Wheaties because they had the pictures of the ballplayers on the back. I had Mel Ott, Carl Hubbell, Hal Schumacher, Danny MacFayden, and Joe Medwick, among others, tacked up on my wall. Not a black ballplayer in the bunch. I do recall that occasionally to "fill the void" I cut out pictures of black ballplayers that appeared in the Amsterdam News *and the* Pittsburgh Courier *and put them up.*

Early black players in the major leagues still remember the indignities they suffered at the hands of hostile managers, teammates, and fans. Sam Jethroe, who joined the old Boston Braves in 1950, describes how his manager Billy Southworth, kept calling him "Sambo" month after month. It was short for "Little Black Sambo," a racist and personally disrespectful epithet. Finally Jethroe, who had decided he'd taken about all he could from Southworth, turned around one day and said right to his face, "My name's not Sambo, it's Sam."

During his first year in the majors in 1950, Jethroe batted .273, hit eighteen home runs, led the National League with thirty-five stolen bases, scored 100 runs, and was named Rookie of the Year. Jethroe continued to play at superstar level in his second year with the Boston Braves and showed all kinds of promise. He belted another eighteen home runs, stole thirty-five bases and again led the league in that category; scored 101 hundred runs, and hit .280. But Jethroe got sick in his third year with the team, and because he was black, he had to play while sick. Remember, niggers had to earn their money on the field, not ailing on the bench. But Sam Jethroe wasn't just a black man on a white man's team, he was an "uppity nigger," whose resistance to racism finally caught up with him. That year, 1952, he only hit thirteen home runs and batted a disappointing .232. Because he had to play while he was sick, he lost his superstar status in the eyes of the Boston management, and they took the opportunity to bounce him right down to the minors after his third season.

No one on his team backed him. Unlike Jackie Robinson he had no player or management support. No "white knight" came to his rescue like Pee Wee Reese did for Jackie in Brooklyn. He could not even become a utility man—like many of the white players on the Braves at that time. Consequently Sam Jethroe was expendable. After spending 1953 in the minor leagues, he finished out his four-year major league career when he played in two games for the Pittsburgh Pirates in 1954. He never even received a pension while white players far beneath his level of talent were allowed to remain in the majors and receive their pensions today.

MONTE IRVIN

MONTE IRVIN: Playing Negro baseball wasn't as bad as a lot of people thought. In other words, we didn't make much money, but we had lots of fun. We played in the summer in the States and then in the wintertime we would go to Puerto Rico, Venezuela, and Mexico, Cuba, Santo Domingo, and Panama. Like that you could wind up in the black, with some money in your pocket, because at the time our aspirations were to buy a house and accumulate something for our families because while we were young fellows and fun-loving and so on, we wanted security for our families. It wasn't nearly as bad as a lot of people said.

> "Well, it wasn't left up to me to put him in there . . . but most of the black ballplayers thought Monte Irvin should have been the first black in the major leagues. Monte was our best young ballplayer at the time. . . . He could do everything. You see, we wanted men who could go there and hit that ball over the fence and Monte could do that. He could hit that long ball, he had a great arm, he could field, he could run. Yes, he could do everything. It's not that Jackie Robinson wasn't a good ballplayer, but we wanted Monte because we knew what he could do. But after Monte Irvin went to the Army and came back, he was sick, and they passed him up and looked for somebody else."
>
> *James "Cool Papa" Bell*

Traveling by bus was rough. It was a thrill for me because I had never done much traveling and we used to go to Rochester, Pittsburgh, and Chicago. I had never been to any of these places and most of the fellows had never been to these places. During the thirties and early forties we were given the chance to travel extensively. So you went in anticipation of seeing something new and most of us on the club felt that way. It wasn't tiring even though the buses weren't that comfortable then. Later on they were when they became air-conditioned. Any time the bus stopped it had to be in a Negro section so that you could be accommodated because at that time you couldn't get served on the highway. You couldn't stay at any of the hotels so consequently we ate out of a bag, so to speak. Cheese and crackers and sardines and tuna fish and milk. We got used to it because it was a way of life.

Say we played an All-Star game or an East-West game in Chicago. We would get paid $50. We might have 53,000 people in the stadium, but you still got paid $50 for that game. But that was $50 more than we had. Salaries at that time averaged maybe $150 to $200 a month. If you made $200, that was a lot of money at that time. Out of that you could save maybe $150, because taxes were very low and so on. We played good ball and had a lot of fun.

There was great rivalry between the white semi-pro clubs and the black teams of the Negro National League and the Negro American League. They would do almost anything to beat us. We beat them more times than they beat us because we actually had strong teams and they would only play on weekends. We played every day. They would squeeze us. By that I mean they had their own umpires and very rarely would they be called out in a crucial situation. They had to swing to actually strike out. Some of our pitchers would throw the ball right down in there on a 3-and-2 count, but very often it was called ball four. What we would do before a game is get together with the umpire and ask him, "What kind of game are we going to have today?" We would tell him that we hoped he wasn't a prejudiced umpire. We would tell him if he was competent he would call it like he saw it. If he was prejudiced then he would squeeze us and we hoped he was not like that, that if he were that way it might cause a lot of trouble and we might not play any more. We decided to do it that way because we had no other recourse and often it would work and he would call it the way he saw it in a crucial situation.

Another trick the white teams used to play when we were at the plate: they would substitute balls that had been put in boxes overnight to deaden them. When *they* were hitting they would switch back to the regular balls. For the most part, however, it was a great rivalry and the games were something to watch.

In the middle thirties none of us thought we would get a chance to play major league ball because the feeling of the country was so intense. In other words, they wouldn't play against us. In fact, earlier there had been All-Star white teams selected to play All-Star black teams, and these All-Star major league teams were beaten most of the time. The commissioner and league president then said there could not be any post-season games where there were more than three major leaguers per squad to compete against a black club. They did not want to be embarrassed because we had some really great ballplayers like Biz Mackey, Ray Dandrige, Roy Partlow, Josh Gibson, Satch Paige, Sam Jethroe, Leon Day, Willy Wells, Joe Green, and Raymond Brown. You should have seen Jethroe then, and at that time I was rated the best Negro prospect. I was the center fielder, ran like a deer, and threw with power. In fact, Josh Gibson told me that when his reign was over he thought that I came close to becoming the "King of Swat."

When I was playing black baseball I could do it all. Like I say, I never saw anybody that could beat me hitting. And I could throw like Willie Mays, Joe DiMaggio, or Carl Furillo. None of them could beat me throwing. I was a consistent hitter, a money hitter. And when the going got tough I could really hit and everybody in major league baseball thought that if I had gotten a real chance, I would have been the first selected black to play major league baseball.

Nineteen thirty-nine. Saw Joe "Ducky" Medwick of the St. Louis Cardinals hit one hell of a homer at the Polo Grounds today. He has to be one of the hardest right-handed hitters I ever saw. But wait a minute! I saw Monte Irvin with the Newark Eagles last week at Ruppert Stadium . . . he could hit the hell out

of the ball. What a ballplayer! Joe Medwick had nothing on him.
Irvin should be in the major leagues.

What happened was I went into the Army and lost my feel
for playing and never got a chance to play. I lost my sharpness
when I came out. I wasn't the same. Hell, I stayed in the Army
for three years. I wasn't the same player when I came out as when
I went in.

I was first approached by the Brooklyn Dodgers in 1945. I
told Rickey at that time, "I'm trying to fight my way back to the
way I used to be and when I get to that point, I'll let you know."
In the meantime, they went ahead and signed Jackie Robinson.
Jackie was signed in 1946 and made the majors in 1947. I just
want to say that they picked an excellent candidate because we
know what he's done. What a great contribution he made! He
might not have been the greatest ballplayer starting out, but he
improved and went ahead to make an excellent record. He was
just a credit to us the way he handled things. He made it much
easier for all of us who came afterwards. Campy, if given an
opportunity earlier, could have stepped right in too.

Campy was a star. He was a star in 1941 and 1942. He started early, but when he polished his skills a little bit, nobody could
touch him. When Josh Gibson was alive and playing, Campy
knew automatically he was the second-string catcher because
Josh was head and shoulders above Campy in every department.
Campy was the first to admit this. They say Babe Ruth had charisma. Well, Josh had the same thing. When he talked to you, you
would like him because whatever he said, he said it a bit differently than anybody else. Josh had that boyish manner about him.
He knew he was the best. He had that quiet kind of confidence.

In 1948 Hank Thompson and I were playing in Cuba. We
both were having great years down there. He was playing for
Havana and I was playing for Alemendares. In Cuba, that's like
the Brooklyn Dodgers playing the Giants. The Giants sent one of

their ace scouts down there, Alex Pompey, to find out whether or
not we would like to play organized baseball. This was the winter
of 1948 and we told them yes. The maximum salary was $5,000,
so we lost money in order to sign, but we knew if we did well and
came up we could make more money in the long run. We came
up, of course.

Hank had been up in 1947 with the Browns. He didn't have
instant success and he was sent down with Willard Brown. When
Hank and I signed with the Giant organization, we spent two or
three months with Jersey City, then we were called up to the Polo
Grounds. I was put on third base, Thompson was put on second
base. Later on he played third and I played first; Leo Durocher
was just experimenting to see where we'd fit. Things finally got
straight when I started playing left field and Hank played third
with Willie Mays in center and Whitey Lockman on first base.
Then we really started to roll.

*On July 8, 1949 at Ebbets Field, Irvin and Thompson were
added to the Giants' lineup for the first time. When Thompson
stepped up in the leadoff spot in the first inning to bat against
Dodger Don Newcombe, it marked the first time in major league
history that a black batter faced a black pitcher. Thompson went
hitless, and Irvin, used later in the game as a pinch hitter, walked
as the Dodgers won 4–3.*

I got a great reception with the Giants. That was two years
after Robinson and Doby. Although Hank Thompson and I were
the first blacks to play with the Giants and there were a lot of
Southerners on the club, they treated us cordially. When I say
Southerners, I'm talking Alvin Dark, Ed Stanky, Whitey Lockman, Don Mueller, Dusty Rhodes, and Johnny Mize.

*Nineteen thirty-seven. Black Yankee manager and pitcher
Bill Holland and I are talking about blacks playing in the big*

leagues. He says, "Son, you and I will never live to see it. Too many Southerners involved in big-league baseball. It just won't happen."

They knew we had ability and all we needed was more experience and confidence. Once we started to come around we were all right. Hank went on to become a fantastic third baseman and I became a pretty good fielder, hitter, and base stealer and had a pretty good career. But you see, I lost ten or twelve good years. I came up at thirty-one years old and played till I was thirty-eight. I would have liked to have come up when I was eighteen or nineteen. I could have made it then. Yes, I'm a little bitter about it. I lost a lot of money and prestige. You're not happy about it but there's nothing you can do. There's no point in being uptight because it'll only hurt you when you feel that way.

My greatest baseball thrill, I would have to say, was the 1951 World Series. I think it was that first day when I got four hits. And I really wanted five. No one has ever gone five for five in a World Series game. The fifth time up I hit a line drive that Yankee first baseman Joe Collins grabbed for the out. I also stole home. I wasn't that fast but I could get the jump on the pitcher. So in the first inning, with two outs and Allie Reynolds pitching for the Yankees, Bobby Thomson was up at the plate and I was on third. Reynolds was taking a long time to deliver the ball. I said to Leo, who was coaching on third, that I thought I could make it. (I'd stolen home five times that season.) I made it easy. I remember Yogi Berra saying, "No, no, no, no, Monte, I got you." I said, "No, no, no you didn't." He said, "How can you tell?" I said, "You'll see it in tomorrow's paper that you missed me."

I think the black player has been the salvation of baseball. Particularly since the National League was the first to sign black players. This is why the National League dominated All-Star competition by winning thirty-seven times between 1950 and

1984. After Ted Williams, Bob Feller, Charles Gehringer, and the rest of those guys went out, then came Willie Mays, Bobby Clemente, Hank Aaron, and Juan Marichal. The National League really took over. This really means a lot because it motivated the Latin American players to come in. And most of them came to the National League too: the Puerto Ricans, the Venezuelans, Santo Dominicans.

Suppose a great star like Willie Mays never got a chance, wouldn't it be a shame? Maybe a man like Josh Gibson would have broken the Babe's record, but Josh never got the chance. Robinson did, Mays did, and Aaron actually broke that record.

Monte Irvin was elected to the Hall of Fame in 1973.

JIM GILLIAM

JIM GILLIAM: I broke in with the Dodgers in 1953. As you know, Jackie started everything for us. He kind of smoothed things over for the young black players of today. I don't think there's as much racial prejudice now as there was when he came up to the Dodgers in 1947. I'm talking about the hotels and the dining rooms or places like that, even in the South. Whereas we used to stay separate from the ball club, we all stay together now. So I think this has been a tremendous stride forward.

One of the greatest things that happened to me or any young black ballplayer was being able to room with Jackie Robinson. We roomed together for about four and a half years. I didn't only get an education on the field, I got it off the field, because if you room with a guy, say for half a year, you're always talking about baseball and things in general and about life and whatnot. Jack gave me a lot of advice that was just invaluable.

As you know, I knew Campanella before Jackie because we came from the same team. I was with the Baltimore Elite Giants, but he was there a little ahead of me and when he used to come to Nashville and play with them, I used to be the bat boy and so I've known Campy for a long time. We've always been close. Campy also gave me a lot of advice about life. These are things I will never forget.

I think one of the greatest highlights of my career was when the Dodgers bought my contract from the Baltimore Elite Giants in 1951 and they sent me to Montreal. Then I was called up to the parent club in 1953 to play with the Campanellas, and the Robinsons, the Reeses, and guys like that; and being named the Rookie of the Year in my first season, and my first World Series when I hit a home run, and to be in seven World Series and win four championships.

I think one of the things that will always stand out in my mind is to have had a manager like Walter Alston for all those years. I was there for twenty-two years or so and I was with him for two years in the minor leagues. I preceded him up here, so our relationship has been wonderful over the years. He's been like a father to me. He was the man who wanted me when my career was just about over and then the front office asked him, "Would you like to have Gilliam?" I think they named him a couple of other players, but he picked me. I have also enjoyed working with the young players, black and white, when I was with the team.

About the old Dodgers: I knew Don Newcombe well and he was a big, happy-go-lucky guy. Everybody thought he was a lazy pitcher, but actually Don was the hardest-working pitcher around. In spring training when I was quite young he used to tell me, "Come on and run with me, man." I used to go out there and run with him for about ten laps and then I would quit. He would just stay out there and run all day. He was a great pitcher, a great competitor, and a very hard worker. He threw hard. He was a hell of a hitter and he helped win a lot of his own ball games with the bat.

Campy was the life of the party. Things never got dull when he was playing. The club could be going a little bad but he would always crack a joke to keep the guys loose. I remember how Campy used to say when the Dodgers were losing and the game was close, "Just let me get one good whack at that guy," and sure enough the guy would make a mistake and Campy would whack the ball right out of there.

But it was a Giant, Willie Mays, who most stands out in my mind. There was absolutely nothing this guy couldn't do. He hit for average, hit for power, and he could throw, steal bases. He could field his position as good as anyone. I would have to say that Willie's the greatest all-around ballplayer that I've ever seen. Of course, Hank Aaron was a great player. I saw him start out with the Braves and every year he got better and better. He was another guy that could do a lot of things on the ball field.

Jim Gilliam died October 8, 1978.

ROY CAMPANELLA

August, 1937. Negro National League four-team double header at Yankee Stadium. Baltimore Elite Giants vs. the Pittsburgh Crawfords. Then the New York Black Yankees vs. the Philadelphia Stars. Eleven-year-old Art Rust, Jr. studies the score card and sees names like Roy Parnell, Philadelphia Stars; Pepper Bassett, Pittsburgh Crawfords; Barney Brown, New York Black Yankees; and Roy Campanella, New York Elite Giants. I said to myself, "What's a 'Campanella?'"

Monday night, shortly before midnight on January 27, 1958. I'm raising a few with Roy Campanella, Don Newcombe, and disc jockey Tommy Smalls at Smalls' Paradise on 135th and Seventh Avenue in Harlem. And Campy says to me, "Man, I don't want to go out to California!" The Dodgers had just completed their last season at Ebbets Field. We were saying good-by. I left them at around one o'clock because a freezing rain was turning New York City streets into glass.

Tuesday morning, January 28, 1958, 7:45 a.m., and I'm on my way to station WWRL to do my sports show and my ears perk up when a news bulletin comes over WJZ. "Roy Campanella in serious accident."

On Tuesday, January 28, 1958 at 3:34 a.m. on a deserted road in Glen Cove, Long Island, Campanella was headed home from Manhattan when his rented Chevy skidded on a sheet of ice on an "S" curve and careened into a telephone pole and overturned. Campanella, pinned in the car for half an hour, suffered fractures and dislocations of the fifth and sixth cervical vertebrae at the neckline. The accident left him paralyzed from the chest down for the rest of his life.

Red Barber bellows from the radio speaker, "The bases are f.o.b. (full of Brooklyns). Dolph Camilli hits a Bedford Avenue Blast (home run). Oh, Doctor!" That "cornpone"-talking guy could really call a ball game. He really painted a picture. Oh, how he used to describe those epic Dodger-Cardinal struggles! Whitlow Wyatt vs. Mort Cooper; Luke Hamlin against Howie Pollet. I used to sit in the farthest corner of the upper left field stands at the Polo Grounds, with no one around me, and actually do the play-by-play—like Barber. A black kid fantasizing.

ROY CAMPANELLA: Well, I started playing in the Negro leagues in 1937. I was still in school in Philadelphia, and I would just play on the weekends with the old Baltimore Elite Giants of the Negro National League. When I started, we received 50 cents a day for meal money. We traveled by bus and we didn't think it was bad. I didn't think it was anything extraordinary because I just wanted to play ball. I was fifteen, and gee how I wanted to play ball. I also wanted to be an architect. That was my goal. I wanted to go to college and major in architecture, but I wanted to play sports, too. I found out that I couldn't do both.

In the old Negro leagues we traveled by bus and car. Some of the stops were pretty good. At the time I was playing with the Baltimore Elite Giants. That was the only team I played with in the Negro National League. There was the Pittsburgh Crawfords in that league with Josh Gibson and Satchel Paige. You'd play in Baltimore one day or that night and be in Pittsburgh the next day. We made this not by plane, not by train, but each team had their own personal bus. We were accustomed to traveling this way. It wasn't always bad, and we always made it.

"The first time I saw Campanella was about 1936. He was about fourteen or fifteen, catching batting practice for the Baltimore Elite Giants. They just carried him around to catch batting practice and he learned how to catch that way. He turned out to be a heck of a catcher, as we all know. But I wouldn't say he was as good as Josh Gibson. He could only do one thing better than Gibson, and that was stay in shape."

Buck Leonard

On the Baltimore team in 1937 we had an outfielder by the name of Bill Wright in left field. Henry Kimbro was in center and another Wright, Zollie, in right field. The two Wrights weren't brothers—they just had the same name. First base, we had a fellow by the name of Jim West, one of the greatest fielding first basemen I ever saw. Second base: Sammy T. Hughes, a tremendous second baseman, in my opinion. At shortstop we came up with a youngster by the name of Tommy Butts, one of the greatest. And I'll go all the way to the big leagues on this: He was one of the greatest shortstops I have had the pleasure of playing with. At third base we had a fellow by the name of Felton Snow, later to become our manager, and a tremendous player. At the time I was a third-string catcher. They had fellows by the names of Biz Mackey, Nish Williams, and myself, and being fifteen years old, it was out of this world playing with these guys. We had a tremendous pitching staff with approximately four starting pitchers and about two reserves and that was it.

I was born and raised in Philadelphia and I went to a mixed school. It was later, when they spoke to my mother and father and asked them to let me play on weekends in the professional Negro league, when I started to realize that blacks could not play in the major leagues and that there was a black big league. That is where I went and played when I was out of school.

Nobody ever believes me, but I didn't know blacks were not playing major league ball until the owners of the Baltimore Elite Giants came to my house and asked my parents to let me play with them on weekends. My attitude hadn't changed about wanting to play ball, but I couldn't understand why blacks couldn't play in the major leagues. Being brought up and raised in Philadelphia and going to an integrated school all my life, and having always played with whites on the football, baseball, basketball, track and field teams, it never really came to be an issue with me. But it did when I found out I couldn't play big-league ball, Being one of the youngest players on our team of the Baltimore Elite Giants, I had this explained to me by the older players and explained in such a way as to show me that none of the white players in any of the other leagues, major or minor, could play any better than we could.

In 1937 there were a lot of black ballplayers who I thought could have made it in the major leagues. One of them—and everyone knows this man's name—was Josh Gibson. I played with Henry Aaron, Willie Mays. I didn't see Babe Ruth, but he established himself as being the greatest home-run hitter in white baseball. Well, knowing Josh Gibson and playing against him, and knowing Henry Aaron and playing against him, too, I think

Josh Gibson was the greatest home-run hitter I have ever seen. Now it's true nobody has ever counted the home runs this man has hit, but I'll say one thing—I'll put him with anybody. Josh Gibson would have been a major league superstar.

The first contact I received from a major league team was when I was playing with the Negro All-Star team at the end of the season in 1945 and at Ruppert Stadium in Newark, New Jersey. This All-Star Negro team was playing a major league All-Star team managed by Charlie Dressen. At the time Charlie Dressen was a coach for the Brooklyn Dodgers and after the game—it was a night game on a Friday night—he stopped me on his way to the third base coaches' box and told me to meet him after the game. Then he asked me to go to the Dodger office that Saturday morning around ten o'clock to talk to Mr. Rickey. I was staying in New York then because I was going to Venezuela to play winter ball afterwards. Jackie Robinson was there, too. I didn't know the way over to Brooklyn, but Mr. Rickey explained to me how to catch the subway and get over there, and I did and had a meeting with him. It was the first time I had ever met Mr. Rickey and he told me that he would like my services but he didn't think it would be for any major league team.

I thought Mr. Rickey was interested in my services for the Brown Dodgers. I told him I was going to Venezuela to play that winter and I'd give him the address where to contact me down there. He asked me, and I can distinctly remember, not to sign a contract with anyone. I told him I wouldn't and he said he would contact me. I told him that I couldn't sign with the Brown Dodgers because at the time I was under contract with Baltimore. So when Mr. Rickey contacted Baltimore, he bought out my contract. That winter when I was playing in Venezuela he asked me to come back to New York. A few days later it was announced the Jackie Robinson had signed with Montreal. Then I started to realize that this was what Mr. Rickey wanted me for. So after we signed I joined the Dodger organization.

At the beginning of the season with Nashua our manager was Walter Alston, who ultimately would manage the Brooklyn and Los Angeles Dodgers for a total of twenty-three years. He was also our first baseman at Nashua and we had a meeting in the clubhouse; he made me feel very much a part of the team. In this meeting, Alston told all the fellows in the club that if he ever got put out of a ball game, I was to run the team. He said he thought that I had more experience than anyone on the team because I had played in the Negro league for fourteen years. Alston got put out of a game in Lawrence, Massachusetts and we were losing by one run in the late innings. I put Don Newcombe in to pinch hit for someone. Newk came through with a home run with a man on base and we won the game by one run. Alston kidded me and said, "You're my manager from now on." I'll never forget that.

Let me say now that the first time that I joined the Dodgers, I'll never forget when I walked through the Dodger door in the clubhouse and one of the Dodger white players greeted me by saying, "Oh, we're saved!" Well, this didn't hit me too good, walking in the door with my bags in my hands and I'm going in the clubhouse and that's exactly what he said to me: "We're saved."

Well, I'm still wondering what that meant but I didn't appreciate it anyhow. Everybody in the clubhouse heard it, including Jackie, but I didn't say anything. I just went in and Leo Durocher, the manager, came out of his office and greeted me. I doubt if Leo heard it, but Leo was a real true guy and a tremendous man. He was the first manager to accept blacks and to go along with them. That's Durocher.

The first black guy I ever played against that was traded from the Dodgers was Joe Black, and this happened in Cincinnati. Holy gee, was I amazed when I walked in the batter's box and they called in Joe Black to pitch to me! Here's a guy I started out with in the Negro leagues and I had always caught him and now I'm batting against him. What am I going to do and what am

I going to look for? It was quite a problem but I worked it out. He had to throw the ball.

It's been rumored that Jackie Robinson and I never got along. Well, we always got along, but we had two different approaches to doing things. Jackie had his way and I had my way. I think we were different individuals, but we were roommates and we were, yes, battling for the same objectives. Jackie was a politician, wanted to be a politician. I didn't. Yes, we were different that way. I would exercise my vote and would advise all blacks to exercise their vote, but I'd be darned if I would go out and get on the soap box and try to preach for one party against another party, for one individual against another individual, but I would definitely exercise my vote. Now Jackie and I didn't see eye to eye on this, but other than that, I thought he was the greatest ballplayer, considering all the obstacles he had to face.

I was so happy to have Jackie as a teammate, and to know him a whole lot better than a whole lot of people. Jackie was a tremendous athlete, and he got better as he went along. He was someone who could take all the riding and different obstacles he had to hurdle over. Nothing could stop this man and the more you would ride him the better he could play. This is the kind of man he was. I lived with Jackie as an athlete and played with him. I could understand what problems he had and what problems I had coming up way back then. It was quite a feat, and I only wish that the youngsters could appreciate that today.

The year is 1938. I'm visiting my aunt in Chicago for the summer. Yankee outfielder Jake Powell is being interviewed on WGN Radio. The interviewer asks Powell what he does in the off season. Powell responded with the following: "I'm a cop in southern Illinois, and I get a lot of pleasure beating up niggers and then throwing them in jail." I remember feeling ill when I heard this. Powell was later fined and then suspended by the Yankee ball club.

I was the first black catcher in the major leagues and as Mr. Branch Rickey told me, "You are going to have to be a diplomat to talk to the ten or eleven different pitchers on this team, to make them use your judgement in calling and giving all the signals. The catcher runs the team in the major leagues, just as a quarterback does on a football team."

My biggest thrill was coming from the Negro National League and being black. I never thought about the Hall of Fame, but after getting in the major leagues and being with these fellows and playing with them all the time, yes, the Hall of Fame is the greatest thing you can accomplish in baseball. This is the highest point in any athlete's life. It's a tremendous tribute and I am so proud and happy that I was able to make it at a young age. And also, a guy that preceded me in the major leagues, Jackie Robinson, who has passed on, but God knows he started all of it. He did. He started all of it.

The black player gave the game something new and I think it put something different in baseball. It made it more of an attraction. This goes for other sports too. It created more enthusiasm in the crowds. More people wanted to come to see the ball games because it was a game that all nationalities could play then. In baseball you have not only the American blacks, but you have the black Cubans, the black Puerto Ricans, the black Venezuelans. Ballplayers from all over the country and the world can participate in major league baseball. This made new fans and made the attendance grow quite a bit. This is what the owners were striving for—more attendance at these games. I think it was a revolution that started in baseball and spread to basketball and to football.

At first the blacks had to dominate to succeed. You just couldn't be ordinary and be a black player and a regular. You had to be a little better than ordinary. A black player had to be better than average. I am going back now to Henry Aaron, Ernie Banks, Jackie Robinson, Don Newcombe. I mean they expected these men to be twenty-game winners and to be .300 hitters and they wanted you at the top of the home-run list, tops in RBI totals. Your Monte Irvins, your Larry Dobys—these men had to excel them. Now it's a little different. Now you can have seven or eight or nine blacks on one team and yes, you can be a substitute. Earlier you didn't see too many black substitutes—either you were a regular or you didn't get on the team. Now there are black substitutes and utility players. This is the big difference in my opinion. In just a matter of a few years, the black has been accepted and he goes all the way now. In other words, now you have acceptance of not only the superstar blacks but the journeyman ballplayers, utility players as well as the superstars.

When we started out in the major leagues to play, we wanted to prove that we could play baseball, to play major league baseball. We were not worried about how much we got to play it. Now the young blacks, before they even sign are worried about how much they are going to get and what type of bonus. Some get tremendous salaries and bonuses, but all of this came about because a number of years ago the first blacks in the leagues wanted to prove that they could play major league baseball and be gentlemen off the field. The uptightness is gone now. All you have to do is have the ability and ask for what you want. And if you don't get it, that's another story.

Roy Campanella was voted into the Baseball Hall of Fame in 1969. He is currently an executive with the Los Angeles Dodgers organization.

DON NEWCOMBE

His repertoire? A hopping fast ball, a low quick-breaking curve, a couple of changeups, and adequate control. His slight wildness was in his favor: It kept the batters loose. His three-quarter overhand delivery was a thing of beauty. He could hit and field. In 1949 he got twenty-two hits, more than any other pitcher, and handled fifty-seven chances without an error.

The first game of the 1949 World Series, Dodgers and Yankees, was a classic. Don Newcombe, the Dodgers' black freshman hurler, and "Chief" Allie Reynolds kept the capacity crowd of fans in Yankee Stadium on the edges of their seats as they dueled 0–0 throughout. Newcombe pitched like an old pro, just as if he had participated in many World Series before. His fastball was hopping and his curve was breaking sharply. As ballplayers would say, "He was throwing aspirin tablets"—the Yankee bats were swinging at air. Reynolds was equally superb.

After eight innings Newcombe had eleven "ks," putting him just two away from the series record of thirteen strikeouts set in 1929 by Athletic right-hander Howard Ehmke. He didn't allow a walk and had given up only four hits to the hard-hitting Yankees.

In the ninth inning Tommy Henrich led off for the Yankees. The great clutch hitter, Henrich, nicknamed "Old Reliable," was facing a top fastball artist, a big man who could blaze the ball in there. Newcombe, who respected Henrich, "worked" him carefully, throwing two balls low and away to the Yankee pull hitter. Newk's third pitch to Henrich was a low curve. Tommy timed it perfectly and "jerked" it into the right-field stands for a heartbreaking 1–0 Yankee victory. Despite the agony and disappointment with the loss of that first game, Newcombe had established himself as one of the best major league pitchers in less than a season.

Despite his size (6-foot-4 and 235 pounds), at times Don Newcombe was accused of being against heavy work. There was a part of his personality that led many to call him lethargic. Born in Madison, New Jersey, on June 14, 1926, Newk started playing baseball at an early age. When he was only nine he pitched batting practice for a semi-pro team. At the age of ten his family moved to Elizabeth, New Jersey, where Newcombe made his niche in football and baseball at Lafayette Junior High. In his senior year in high school Newcombe quit and joined the Army. When he got out of the service in 1943 he had a tryout with the Newark Eagles, impressed the owners, Mr. and Mrs. Abe Manley, and was signed to a contract. Besides a blazing fastball, he also owned a pretty good curve and he was one hell of a hitter. That year he won seven and lost five. In 1945 he won fourteen and lost only four.

In October 1945, he pitched an All-Star game at Ebbets Field. One team was composed of Negro National League stars, the other of major leaguers such as Whitey Kurowski, Frank McCormick, Eddie Stanky, Buddy Kerr, and Ralph Branca. He pitched impressively against the big leaguers. After the game Brooklyn coach Clyde Sukeforth told Newcombe, "Mr. Rickey wants to talk to you." Subsequently, Newcombe signed with the Brooklyn organization and was offered to the Danville Club of the Three-I League. Danville rejected the offer, as they had done to Roy Campanella previously. No blacks were wanted. So Don, with Campy, went to Nashua, where he won fourteen and lost four, duplicating his Negro National League record. The following season he was 19-and-6 for Nashua, striking out 186 batters in 223 innings. His wins and strikeouts were tops in the New England league.

In the winter of 1947 Newcombe played winter ball for the Caracas, Venezuela, club managed by Roy Campanella. There he was 10-and-3. In 1948 he was promoted to Montreal, where he won seventeen and lost six, posted a 3.14 earned-run average, and struck out 144 batters in 189 innings. In 1949 he joined the Dodgers and became an important member of the pennant-winning club, winning seventeen games against eight losses, striking out 149 batters in 244 innings and posting a 3.17 earned-run average. During a hot stretch in the pennant fight Newk hurled thirty-two consecutive scoreless innings. He was honored as National League Rookie of the Year. Newk won five awards and was the only major league pitcher to have won both a Cy Young and an MVP.

DON NEWCOMBE: I was the first black pitcher ever to take the mound in a major league World Series game. At the time I remember I had a double set of feelings: a modicum of fear about the Yankee dynasty we were playing and that I was only a rookie.

The Yankees had instilled fear in everybody in the American League all year. And I was a novice who had to pitch in the most important game of the year against the most powerful club in baseball. But when I started warming up I didn't feel that fear. With Jackie Robinson and Roy Campanella being there, I had confidence. They just said, "Go out and throw it, big fella. Let's see what happens." And that's just what I did. You see, they helped take the pressure off.

It had only been five years earlier, when I was seventeen, that I was a starting pitcher with the Newark Eagles. I didn't have a dream back in 1944 that I would be pitching against the Yankees in the 1949 series. Back in 1944 there was no way that a kid from the ghetto in Elizabeth, New Jersey, could ever think along those lines. In fact, I never even had a baseball idol other than Satchel Paige. And there was I was playing against him. I didn't idolize a Joe DiMaggio or a Hank Greenberg or one of those players in organized baseball as other youngsters did because I could never hope to be like them.

Things began changing for me in 1945 when I played at Ebbets Field in an All-Star game. On one team were the Negro League All-Stars and on the other team were the major leaguers. I remember it was cold and windy on the field. It was raining that day also. But none of that bothered us because we wanted to play for the fans, the 10,000 people in the stands of whom most were black folks wanting to see a black All-Star team hold their own against the best of the majors. The big-leaguers had beaten us the first two games. Ralph Branca had shut us out in Newark on a Friday night and they had beaten us again on Saturday. We wanted to play Sunday because we saw a chance to make a few bucks.

I started that third game for the Negro League All-Stars. I was doing pretty well against the major league batters, but I hurt my arm in the third inning and had to be taken out. I remember how bad I felt about it. I went into the clubhouse and sat there in the darkness all by myself and I began to cry. I believed my baseball career was all over. I was only eighteen years old at the time and you can imagine my trepidation and worry about my future as a ballplayer. I didn't hear his footsteps at first, but into the clubhouse walked a white man named Clyde Sukeforth who was at that time the chief scout for the Brooklyn Dodgers. But I didn't know who he was. I just looked up at this white man with this great big hat on and thought to myself that I never saw such a big hat in my whole life on such a small man. Sukeforth asked me if my name was Don Newcombe. I nodded.

"What are you crying about?" he said to me as if he knew something that I didn't.

"Well, I just hurt my arm out there and I guess my career is over," I answered.

He asked, "What makes you think that?" I didn't know what to say. Then he said, "I'm Clyde Sukeforth and I'm with the Dodgers and I work for Mr. Branch Rickey, who owns the Dodgers."

"Who's Mr. Rickey?" I asked him. Mr. Sukeforth said, "He's the owner of the Dodgers and he's thinking of starting a Negro team to play at Ebbets Field while the white team is on the road. They're going to be called the Brown Dodgers." He explained that he had a few other black players under contract and he wanted to know if I would be interested in talking to Mr. Rickey about playing for him.

"Sure, if he is going to pay me some money," I said right back to him.

Then Mr. Sukeforth smiled and said, "Sure he'll pay you. Why don't you come back over to Ebbets Field. Go to Montague Street to the Dodger home office and talk to Mr. Rickey tomorrow morning."

This conversation took place late on a Sunday afternoon in the Ebbets Field clubhouse. I had to be back in Mr. Rickey's office the next morning. But that's what he wanted and that's what I did; I came back over from Newark, where I was staying at the time, spoke to Mr. Rickey the next morning, and he signed me to a contract in the Dodger organization.

I spent the next few years in the minor leagues. I couldn't play at Danville in the Three-I League because the president of the league said he didn't want any black players—he used a different word to describe me—and threatened that if "you send any of them down here, we're going to close the league." Mr. Rickey called Buzzie Bavasi who managed the Dodger team in Nashua, New Hampshire. That was the only Dodger team that Roy Campanella and Don Newcombe could have played on because at that time it was the lowest classification. The higher classifications were all in the South and the West where they didn't want blacks in the first place. Mr. Rickey called Buzzie on the phone and asked if he would take these two Negro players on his team. And Buzzie wanted to know if we could play baseball. Mr. Rickey said, "I think so because I've signed them to contracts." Buzzie said: "Send them up. We don't care what color they are." And to this day I wonder if Buzzie had turned us down or if Walter Alston turned us down whether you would have ever seen Roy Campanella and Don Newcombe play professional baseball.

I almost blew my first year in the National League by jumping the Montreal club and going home. I didn't understand Mr. Rickey's strategy in not bringing me and the other players up. I was pretty young, not willing to wait, and I became frustrated. I remember that I had been sent back to Montreal after pitching some pretty good games against the Dodgers in spring training. I felt good about the pitching, but I was still sent back to Montreal. I was terribly disappointed that I wasn't brought up to the Dodgers as I had expected I would be after my pitching performance. I didn't understand what Mr. Rickey was doing. He had a stair-step plan, he called it, a step-by-step procedure he was using to move us up to the majors. He wanted Jackie Robinson first and then Roy to become firmly entrenched on the team and in the minds of the fans. Then if he felt there was a need for me on the team, he would bring me up. I didn't know that at the time and I jumped the Montreal club and headed home to New Jersey.

I stayed home three days and then called Buzzie Bavasi in Montreal to ask him if he would take a damn fool back on his ballclub. I was sorry. I had made a mistake. And he said that if that damn fool can come up and win him twenty games, just send him back. I returned to Montreal, started the season, and pitched two good games: a shutout, I think, and then a one-run game against the Newark Bears. Then I lost the next two games by only one run each. But these were four pretty good baseball games in which I thought I showed a lot of control. I believed, after pitching those games, that I really should have been brought up by the Dodgers.

I began to get down on myself and I couldn't understand what was going on in Mr. Rickey's mind. I wish I could have understood, but I was young and I didn't know what he was thinking. I remember I was feeling pretty low, and then one day around the middle of May, Buzzie Bavasi called me down to his ballpark where, with a completely straight face on, he asked me, "How long will it take you to get home, pack whatever you need, pick up your wife, and meet Mr. Rickey at Roosevelt Field in Long Island to fly to Chicago where you'll join the Dodgers?"

"You're crazy, you're kidding me," I said, but I didn't wait around for him to answer. I drove my car home from Montreal to Elizabeth, New Jersey, where I lived and then headed out the following day to meet Mr. Rickey over at Roosevelt Field to join the Dodgers. We had to fly his plane out. We stopped in Harrisburg, Pennsylvania, to pick up Billy Cox who they had just acquired through a trade, and then met the ballclub in Chicago. I thought that was the happiest day of my life.

But the happiest part of the day was when I walked into the hotel where the Dodgers were staying and straight into Jackie's and Roy's room where they were sitting at a table having dinner. I said to myself, "Here I am, part of the team with Jackie and Roy." I was never happier in my life. I felt I'd truly accomplished something. The next day I got on the bus for the game at Wrigley Field and the team gave me number 36 with DODGERS written across the chest. I thought I was the biggest guy in the world.

My feelings of accomplishment stayed with me for the next few months. However, I soon found out that even though I was now in the majors, times were still tough. I realized that black players still had to fight for their rights. This became particularly obvious to me after I got out of the Army and returned to the Dodgers where it all came to a head one night at the Chase Hotel in Mound City in St. Louis in 1954.

The story behind the incident in St. Louis actually started in 1947 when Jackie first joined the Dodgers and had to have special hotel accommodations whenever the team went to St. Louis. Because of segregation, Jackie couldn't stay with his teammates and had to go to another hotel, a substandard hotel, in a "different" part of town. During the years before 1954, we had to endure a lot of hardship because of this segregation, especially because the accommodations at the hotel where we stayed were far worse than the Chase Hotel where the rest of the team stayed. The Chase had air conditioning—always important in the summer St. Louis heat. Our hotel rooms had no air conditioning at all and the heat would wear us out by the time we had to play. Also, we had to eat this substandard food that was actually making us sick.

We had to get off our train in St. Louis and get our own suitcases, find a taxi cab in the mornings, and go to this substandard hotel. The other players on our team would get on an air-conditioned bus; they didn't even have to touch their shaving kits unless they wanted to. Then they'd go to the Chase Hotel which was air-conditioned, luxurious, and beautiful. Jackie had been putting up with this on his own since 1947. Later Dan Bankhead got there and after him Roy Campanella and eventually myself. We could never figure out why no one spoke up for us. We were all on the same team, we should have had the same accommodations. It was getting to the point where we knew things had to change, but we didn't know how or when.

Finally, by 1954, I'd put up with about as much as I could take. I'd served in the military in 1952 and 1953 to fight for my country and lost two years out of my career. But America was in a war and we had to do our part—at least that's what I believed. When I got out of the service, I rejoined the Dodgers and renewed my career with enthusiasm.

I was also looking for change. I said to Jackie Robinson one day in St. Louis after we had been separated from the team and sweating it out in our special hotel, "Jackie, I'm not going to live like this any longer. I've just spent two years in the Army fighting for my flag, for my country. I'm not going to live like a substandard human being any more unless somebody can tell me why I've got to live like that. I think it's been long enough."

"Newk, you're right," Jackie said. "Let's go to the hotel where the rest of the team is and find out why we can't stay there." We asked Roy Campanella if he wanted to come along, but he said, "No, I'll stay here until you get back."

We didn't wait around any longer. Jackie and I hailed a cab and rode over to the Chase Hotel. We walked in the front door looking for the manager of the place. Now, there are a lot of different versions about what went on, but I was there and I'm telling you that this is the way it really happened.

Jackie and I found the manager right away. He knew who we were. He took us into the dining room of the hotel and bought us a cup of coffee because he was a very generous man. And Jackie said to him, "Listen, do you know why we're here? Don and I want to know something."

"Yes," the manager said. "I know exactly why you're here. You want to know why you can't stay in this same hotel with your teammates."

As God is my witness, here is what the man said: "The only reason we don't want you staying here, or didn't want you staying here all these years is that we didn't want you using the swimming pool."

"My God," Jackie said. "What are you talking about? I don't know how to swim." In fact, Jackie knew how to do everything, but he sure didn't want that man to know he could swim.

"I don't swim during the baseball season," I said to the manager, following Jackie's lead. "I'm afraid to hurt my arm."

The manager looked at the two of us, nodded, and said, "Okay, it's all right then. You can move in, but just don't go in the swimming pool."

When we moved into that hotel, he made sure, that manager did, that we never even had a chance to look at the swimming pool because he put us on the opposite side of the hotel from the swimming pool. He put us so far away we could never even get a chance to look at what was going on. I still don't know what his concerns were. Maybe he didn't want us looking at those pretty white women walking around the pool deck with all their bikinis on. But he didn't know me. If I wanted to look at something pretty, something beautiful, I was going to look at it whether he segregated me or not. Eventually Jackie, I, and Roy Campanella moved into all the hotels with the team on a regular basis and incidents like these became part of baseball lore.

But the important thing about this incident for me is that it was one of many things that Jackie Robinson did to stand up for his rights. I was glad I happened to be there alongside him. It took a lot of courage at a time when too few people had courage. I tell many youngsters, particularly younger ballplayers, not to forget what Jackie Robinson did. There are too many people playing baseball today who have forgotten what Jackie Robinson, Roy Campanella, Satchel Paige, Larry Doby, and even what Don Newcombe did.

They have forgotten that we made it possible for them to play in the big leagues and earn the kinds of salaries clubs are paying today. I'm very dismayed about that because it's as if a piece of history is being set aside. Therefore, I tell whoever I speak to: Don't ever forget Jackie Robinson. Don't forget a piece of American history. Similarly, I don't think that baseball should be allowed to forget Jackie in any way. I would even promote a national holiday for Jackie Robinson to keep his name and story in the minds of people, especially the young people, because of the contributions he made to our national sport. Baseball belongs to everybody because of the courage of Jackie Robinson.

I remember vividly having dinner at my house one night in 1968 with a very, very wonderful, famous man who sat at our table. "Don," he said. "You and Jackie and Roy will never know how easy you made it for me to do my job."

His job was civil rights, and that man was Dr. Martin Luther King, Jr. One month later he was killed on a hotel balcony in Memphis because he had a dream and he believed in something the way Jackie believed in something. There was Martin Luther King back in the 1950s and 1960s having police dogs set on him and having fire hoses shot at him and taking abuse. He was even thrown in jail for what he believed in. But he said in 1968 that Jackie, Roy, and I made it possible for him to do his job. Suppose that it was Martin doing the same job he did in 1947 the way Jackie did his job. Where would Martin Luther King be? Would he have made it to 1968? I doubt it. That's why Jackie Robinson is so important to me, to baseball, and to all Americans.

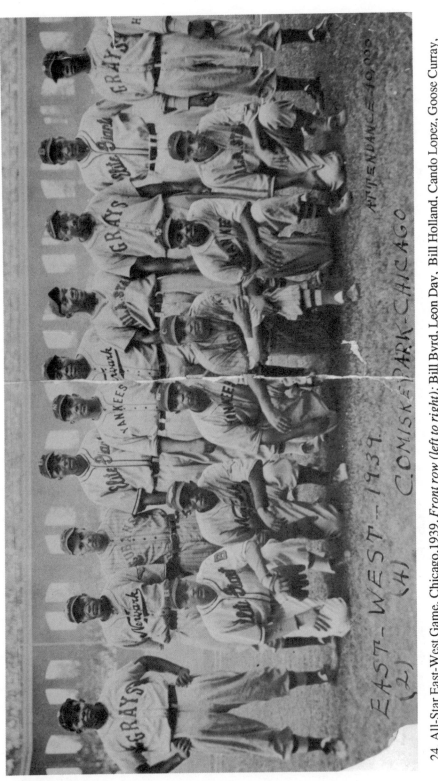

24. All-Star East-West Game, Chicago, 1939. *Front row (left to right):* Bill Byrd, Leon Day, Bill Holland, Cando Lopez, Goose Curray, Red Parnell. *Back row (left to right):* Buck Leonard, Willie Wells, Jose Fernandez, Sammy Hughes, George Scales, Mule Suttles, Pat Patterson, Josh Gibson, Bill Wright, Ray Partlow. *Walter (Buck) Leonard Collection.*

25. Newark Eagles, 1945. *Top (left to right)*: Monte Irvin, Fred Wilson, Len Pearson, Mule Suttles, Max Manning, Harry Cozart, Ed Stone, James Brown, Johnny Hayes. *Bottom:* Leon Day, Dick Seay, Dick Lundy, Willie Wells, Leon Ruffin, Jimmy Hill, Vernon Riddick. *Max Manning.*

26. Jackie Robinson with the Montreal Royals of the International League in 1946.
National Baseball Library, Cooperstown, N.Y.

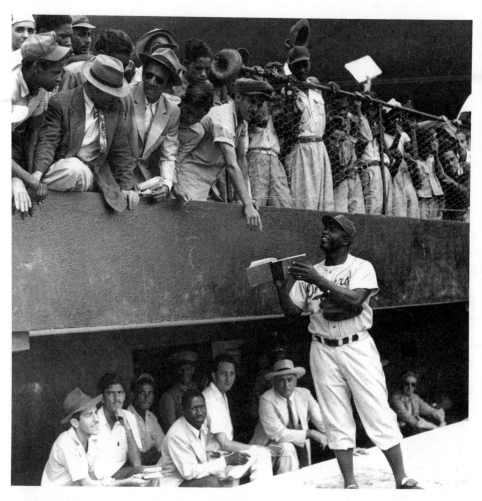

27. Jackie Robinson, signing autographs in Havana, Cuba, spring training, 1947.

28. Jackie Robinson with the Brooklyn Dodgers in his rookie year, 1947. *National Baseball Library, Cooperstown, N.Y.*

29. Jackie Robinson and Branch Rickey having a chat.

30. Jackie Robinson, as a second baseman, is shown leaping and throwing to first to complete a double play against the Phillies at Ebbets Field in 1950. *Wide World Photos.*

31. Seen here in a Montreal Royals uniform, pitcher Dan Bankhead joined the Brooklyn Dodgers and Jackie Robinson on August 25th, 1947, to become the second black on the ball club. *National Baseball Library, Cooperstown, N.Y.*

32. John Wright, a twenty-seven-year-old right-handed pitcher who played with the Newark Eagles, Pittsburgh Crawfords, and the Homestead Grays. He played on the 1946 Montreal Royals with Jackie Robinson to become the second African-American in organized baseball in modern times. *National Baseball Library, Cooperstown, N.Y.*

33. On the Fourth of July, 1947, Bill Veeck of the Cleveland Indians announced that he had purchased from the Newark Eagles of the Negro League a twenty-two-year-old infielder named Larry Doby who became the first black on the Cleveland Indians and the first black in the American League. *National Baseball Library, Cooperstown, N.Y.*

34. Sam Jethroe, speedy outfielder of the Boston Braves, who led the National League in steals in 1951, with 35. On April 18th, 1950, he became the first black on the Boston Braves. *National Baseball Library, Cooperstown, N.Y.*

35. Sam Hairston. First black with the Chicago White Sox in 1951. *National Baseball Library, Cooperstown, N.Y.*

36. Second baseman Curt Roberts played his first game with the Pittsburgh Pirates on April 13, 1954, to become the first African-American on the roster.

37. Right-handed pitcher Bob Trice. In 1953 he became the first black with the Philadelphia Athletics. *National Baseball Library, Cooperstown, N.Y.*

38. Joe Black of the Brooklyn Dodgers. When he beat the New York Yankees 4–2 in Game One of the 1952 World Series, he became the first black pitcher to win a Series game. *National Baseball Library, Cooperstown, N.Y.*

39. Emmet Ashford, the first black umpire in major league baseball. He officiated in the Pacific Coast League from 1954 to 1965, and then in the American League from 1966 to 1970. He worked the 1967 All-Star game and the 1970 World Series. He died March 1, 1980. *National Baseball Library, Cooperstown, N.Y.*

40. Emmet Ashford in action. *Emmet Ashford collection.*

41. San Francisco Giants slugger Willie Mays shows his batting form in the eighth inning of the 1959 All-Star Game in Pittsburgh. He walloped a tremendous triple to right center that won the game for the National League. *Wide World Photos.*

42. Willie Mays, one of the greatest all-around players in the history of baseball. In his 22 years in the bigs, he had 3,283 hits, 660 home runs, and a .302 average.

43. Willie Mays bids adieu. The New York Mets' outfielder tips his hat to the fans for the last time during farewell ceremonies for him at home plate in New York's Shea Stadium, September 26, 1973. The Mets added to Mays' sendoff by downing the Expos 2–1. *Wide World Photos.*

44. Leroy (Satchel) Paige, then with the Kansas City A's. *The Baseball Commissioner's Office.*

45. Satchel Paige, Negro pitcher signed July 7, 1948, by the Cleveland Indians, talks with Bob Feller in the dugout before the game with Chicago. *Wide World Photos.*

46. Leroy "Satchel" Paige was black baseball in the 1930s and early 1940s. He was the Babe Ruth of the black leagues in the sense that he had the charisma, that something that filled the coffers, in many instances. He was "the franchise" for some of the Negro clubs. *National Baseball Library, Cooperstown, N.Y.*

The Record Breakers

ERNIE BANKS

Ernie Banks was a thin shortstop weighing only 150 pounds who was purchased from the Kansas City Monarchs for a reported $25,000. He said he was frightened and really didn't get over it, didn't feel confident of himself, until about 1958 and 1959 when he won the National League's Most Valuable Player award in successive years.

ERNIE BANKS: Do I remember my first homer for the Cubs? I certainly do. It was in old Sportsman's Park in St. Louis, off Gerry Staley, September 20th, 1953. The pitch? A knuckleball that hung inside.

I enjoyed black baseball very, very much. I played with some outstanding men when I was with the Kansas City Monarchs. Men like Gene Baker, Connie Johnson, who was formerly with the White Sox; Curt Roberts, who played for the Pittsburgh Pirates, Barney Sorrell . . . a lot of great players who were playing at that time and in the early fifties, and I remember those days extremely well. They were very important to me in my life as a baseball player. We played fine baseball in the Negro League. We played good defense, had all-around good hitting . . . it was real heads-up type baseball. We had a tremendous love for the game and were happy to be together and represent the Kansas City Monarchs. We traveled by bus. It was tough, but we had a lot of fun. We kind of enjoyed that camaraderie on the bus, in the hotels, in the ballparks. It was an all-around, well-balanced life and a great experience . . . an awful lot of fun. I really enjoyed it.

The first major league teams to show interest in me were the Cardinals and the White Sox. I was never aware of it until I was signed by the Cubs, but at that time I didn't know the scouts who were following me. A guy by the name of Downing, who was in Chicago, followed me for the White Sox, and another scout by the name of Quincy Troupe scouted me for the Cardinals. I didn't know this at the time. I was just playing and enjoying it, and I wasn't thinking about playing in the major leagues or signing with any specific organizations. But after I signed with the Cubs I met these men, and they told me they had followed me for more than a month to sign me with the White Sox or the St. Louis Cardinals.

When I joined the Cubs in 1953 I got tremendous treatment. First of all, I joined the Cubs from Pittsburgh, where I played my last game with the Kansas City Monarchs, and I flew into Chicago where I was met by one of our coaches, Ray Johnson, at the airport. He took me to the hotel. That impression was a good one because it showed me they cared. It showed me they were concerned and that they wanted me.

After I arrived at the ballpark the following morning, I had a chance to meet my good friend Gene Baker, who signed with the Cubs the same time I did. We met and we talked for the first time. He kind of guided me to my locker and the players on the team and introduced me to the players, because he had met them in spring training of 1953. Of course, Yosh Kawano, our equipment manager, introduced me to everybody. The Cub manager at that time was Phil Cavaretta. He came out and introduced himself. Everybody was warm and candid. They let me know what I was supposed to do on that particular day: go out and take infield and batting practice, run around the bases, the usual bit you tell young players when they first arrive on a club.

Gene Baker and I worked pretty close together. We hung together and actually did everything together on the field. I kind of followed him because he had much more experience than I did in baseball. So it was a great, warm cordial feeling in Chicago. A lot of fine people, great people, great players like Ralph Kiner, who's now with the New York Mets broadcasting, Hank Sauer, Frankie Baumholtz, Paul Minner, Dee Fondy, and a lot of players I remember so well and still see who were very nice to me. When I went out on the field, the fans' response was tremendous for Gene Baker and me.

The ballplayer, black or white, who had the greatest influence on my career was, I would say, Gene Baker, because we were together in Chicago for more than five years. He had the experience—he played in the Pacific Coast League for five years and had great years there. He was an outstanding player, a great student of baseball with a lot of instinct for the game and for people. He had a tremendous business mind as far as contracts were concerned—what to sign and what to do. Just being with him was a tremendous influence on my baseball career. Of course, Jackie Robinson was playing when I came up. I'll always remember that he was one of the first players on the Dodgers to come over and wish me well. He told me a few things . . . to play hard and do the best I can. I was very appreciative of that. I'll always remember Jackie as the man who gave me great inspiration when I started with the Cubs.

As for some other highlights of my career, there have been such things as setting marks and records that created an image for us so that we can be in the Hall of Fame. The MVP award was one award that I'm truly proud of. I won it two years in a row, 1958 and 1959. There were the fielding records for shortstops in 1959, five grand slam home runs in one season, hitting more homers than any other shortstop in the majors for one season (forty-seven in 1958). Playing in twelve All-Star games was certainly a great thrill . . . to be associated with great players like Willie Mays, Hank Aaron, Stan "The Man" Musial, Duke Snider, Jim Gilliam, and Jackie Robinson, and all the other great players in the National League. Hitting a home run in the All-Star game in Kansas City where I started back in 1951 certainly was a great thrill.

Since I was in the big leagues, there has been a tremendous amount of great ballplayers, but the guy who stood head and shoulders above them all was Willie Mays. He was so exciting, not only exciting to the fans, but to the teams he played with— the Giants—and against. He was just amazing. Overall, Hank Aaron has had a tremendous influence on my life as far as success and balance are concerned. He's done a lot of great things in his career and is still doing a lot of things. He understands people, he accepts people. He always remembered the route he took, when he came up. He has a tremendous feel for people. He has never forgotten that people are the ones that make us what we are. He is that type of player.

As far as the winning attitude is concerned and my career, Roberto Clemente was the player who gave me that winning-type feeling, that winning is the thing, winning is the only thing. To strive to win and be best. He made a great impression on me as far as winning is concerned, because I'd never been on a winner and he had. He would explain the ingredients of being a winner. "Preparation meets opportunity"—that was Roberto's basic philosophy. You've got to prepare yourself and when the opportunity comes take command of it. Those three fellows had a tremendous influence on me. Of course, I can't leave out Jackie Robinson—withstanding all the outside aggravation and still being able to play outstanding baseball and being a man of history too is a great inspiration.

I was very fortunate in the big leagues regarding treatment. I had not had any real problems, derogatory remarks, or hostility.

One thing you have to understand is that everyone is not going to like you. You have to understand that at the beginning. In fact, Aaron and I used to talk about this at the beginning of our careers, that you should try to get along with the majority of the people.

A lot of fans have asked me who's the toughest pitcher I had to face in the majors. I would say Don Newcombe. He had tremendous drive. He loved competition, was a winning-type pitcher. He was the type of man that had great natural ability. He could throw a ball hard. He had great control, and he could hit like hell; he was the type of man everybody would like to be like. Newk was a winner. He occasionally would talk to his competitors, but most of the time he was just preparing himself mentally.

Newk would visit and talk but once he got on that mound he was a monster. Newk was tough because for two and a half hours he had the ability to concentrate on that mound. Nothing could distract him. He had complete concentration. Fans might say something, time might be called, balls might roll on the field, or hecklers from the other bench might try to get to him. He never let anything distract him from his ultimate goal, namely getting the batter out and winning. He worked extremely hard to keep himself in tip-top shape. He ran all the time he wasn't pitching. He was completely dedicated to the game of baseball. I would come to the ballpark and look out there and here was a top pitcher like Newcombe running, running.

He was an amazing athlete. Every time I faced Don Newcombe it was always a tough day for me and the Cubs. He had explosive speed and a big, jug-handle curve. We knew Newk would be right there throwing that ball as hard as he could. He was one of the very few players that I knew of who pitched a double-header. That shows the strength, stamina, and determination of the man. I think that this is one thing you won't see for a long time in baseball: someone pitching a double-header.

Fergie Jenkins was another great pitcher. Jenkins and I roomed together when he first joined the Cubs in the early sixties, and he knew he could pitch, despite his difficulties in Philadelphia. He was a reliever then and did a fine job in that role. One day we were playing in Atlanta and manager Leo Durocher decided to give him a starting chance. He went out there and pitched a shutout against the Braves. The Braves had a lot of "stick" on that team: Hank Aaron, Rico Carty, Orlando Cepeda, among others. Fergie went out there and pitched so beautifully and so easily, it really opened up everybody's eyes to the fact that he could start.

Afterwards I asked him about the game and some of the things he thought about while he was out on the mound. He said he was thinking about what they said about him in Philadelphia, that he couldn't pitch, didn't have a good-enough fastball, and that he should be a relief pitcher. That stayed on his mind and gave him the drive and determination to go out there and win and prove to the people that he could win. And boy, did he do that! He had six twenty-game seasons with the Chicago Cubs and one with the Texas Rangers.

The most important thing that has gotten away from me? That's playing in a World Series. I'm sorry that eluded me during my career.

Ernie Banks was elected to the Baseball Hall of Fame in 1977.

ELSTON HOWARD

ELSTON HOWARD: Not too many people know this, but in 1967 Bill Veeck attempted to buy the Washington Senators' franchise and name me as the manager. It was the year I was playing with the Red Sox. I met Veeck on the elevator in the Jefferson Hotel in St. Louis (Boston Red Sox–St. Louis Cardinals World Series) and he asked me would I join him for breakfast. We started to talk, and he asked me if I would be interested in managing a ballclub. When he said that to me I was shocked and I said, "What are you talking about?" And he said, "I've been negotiating to buy the Washington Senators." But later the deal fell through. Bob Short bought the ballclub and Veeck went into the race-horse business at Suffolk Downs in Boston. So in other words, the deal never did come off. But he had offered me the job. He was going to let me name all my coaches and run the ballclub, which I wanted full power to do. If I managed a ballclub—and I would say he had often talked to me about it, but I would never bring it out because it was between ourselves—I would continue playing and once in a while would spell the other catcher in a double-header. In other words, I wanted to play and manage, like Lou Boudreau. I was to get a three-year contract, and that was the whole deal.

I would say that one of the big problems of managing a ballclub is communicating with the men. I think that the big problem is you have twenty-five men and you can't satisfy all of them. I think they have only one thing in mind, and that is to win.

When I came to this ballclub—the Yankees—being the first black player here, I didn't have any problems. I had more problems attempting to stay in hotels. I had no problems with the ballplayers. Phil Rizzuto was like a father to me. Hank Bauer, Yogi Berra, Andy Carey, all these fellows were trying to make my season a very happy and successful one with the New York Yankees.

The Yankee managerial job was never offered to me. There never was any thought of it at all. Gabe Paul told me they wanted somebody with experience and this is something that always arises when you get into the problem of a black manager: wanting somebody with managing experience. I say again that it is overrated. You get a lot of experience when you're playing the game, and especially me being a catcher and working with pitchers, I think I have just as much experience as anybody, and I've been around as long as a lot of the ballplayers. But the whole thing you hear over and over again is the bullshit experience thing.

When I joined the Yankee club in spring training of 1955, I had a big problem because I couldn't stay in the hotel in St. Petersburg. I give two guys a lot of credit: Dan Topping and Del Webb. They said the club is moving out and going to Ft. Lauderdale where I could stay in the hotel. So after that the season opened. In Kansas City and Chicago they wouldn't serve me in the restaurants until Stengel raised hell. Stengel told the hotel, "We came as a ballclub and Elston Howard is part of the ballclub. If he can't be accommodated, we'll leave." I never heard anything nasty raised from any of the other ballclubs, because if I had there would have been a fight. I just couldn't have taken what Jackie took. I was born in St. Louis and I came up in the ghetto areas. Any time I heard a man say "nigger" or "black so-and-so," I was ready to fight.

The players on the Yankees were good to me, especially Phil Rizzuto. Phil did everything. He would call me up and say, "Let's go to the movies." Andy Carey, Hank Bauer, Mickey Mantle, Gene Woodling, Gil McDougal—they all worked with me and knew what I was going through, and they went out of their way to help. But Phil Rizzuto was the most important of them all. To this day I will never forget what he did for me when I first came up. He made everything possible for me to be a happy person. We would get into a town like Chicago and he would say, "What are you doing? Let's go out." This man really kept me together. I wanted to play winning baseball, and if you had a lot on your mind you couldn't do this. Rizzuto kept my head together. I call him the "great white father" because he is a hell of a guy.

I started playing baseball in St. Louis in sandlots, and I played in high school and had about forty some scholarships to go to college. I had three in the big ten—Illinois, Michigan, and Michigan State—to play football. I had nine for baseball. I went to a little college in St. Louis for one semester, Stowe Teachers College, and I dropped out and went to play with the Kansas City Monarchs in the Negro American League. My roommate there was Ernie Banks. Later on he went up to the big leagues. Willard Brown and Hank Thompson also played on that club when I got there. So I was a young kid just graduated from school. Later on Willie Mays was in the league. We played against each other when we were very young, but the leagues were great. It was tough traveling around, but I didn't mind it at the time because I was young and I liked it. We would play sometimes two games a day and jump from St. Louis all the way into New York for a game. It wasn't comfortable in the bus, but we had a good ballclub and we played very good baseball.

It meant something to me playing in the black leagues, and I saw a lot and I enjoyed every bit of it. Many of the people in the leagues helped me—like Teeny Edwards, a black man out of St. Louis—and they had good baseball knowledge. When Jackie Robinson came up, I had one thing in mind, to play major league ball. Everything opened up, and baseball was my life from the sandlots and high school right through to the black leagues. Then the Yankees bought my contract along with Frank Bowen's and we went from the minor leagues to the majors.

Despite what many people say, I never had the feeling that the Yankees really didn't want to bring me up. When I got there they had a guy behind the plate by the name of Yogi, which means I had to play the outfield, although I was a catcher when I was with Toronto and I had won the Most Valuable Player award in the International League. No, they didn't stall me in any way. Stengel put me in the outfield, and I was glad to get into the lineup and make the ballclub, for the simple reason that Yogi was the Most Valuable Player when I came up and he was one of the best catchers in baseball.

Yogi and Roy Campanella were the best I ever saw in baseball, and those two fellows were right in the prime of their careers. I couldn't move Yogi from behind the plate because he was an outstanding ballplayer. I settled for playing left field, first base, and I spelled Yogi behind the plate. Stengel said I was his four-way man and sometimes I would get mad because I moved around so much and a lot of ballclubs wanted me, but I'm very glad my career started here. As far as the plight of the black ballplayer is concerned, I think that baseball's ownership owes executive jobs to the top black ballplayers in the majors, like Henry Aaron. These ballplayers need a lot more respect.

Regarding some of my career highlights, I think my biggest thrill was when I played in my first game with the Yankees. We were up in Boston and Stengel would go with the percentages. Fenway Park had that short left-field fence, so he put me in the lineup and I went out and got 5-for-5. That was one of my greatest thrills. Then of course, that year we got into the World Series and I played against big Don Newcombe, who was an outstanding pitcher at the time. My first time up against him at the Yankee Stadium I hit a home run. This was the first time a rookie had hit a home run in a World Series his first time up.

Of course, making the All-Star teams and being selected the Most Valuable Player—the first black MVP in the American League in 1963—and later on being the first black coach in the American League, these were some of my greatest moments. Those were some of the thrills of playing baseball and being on so many winners with the Yankees—and having a good relationship with the players. I was thrilled to be playing with some great ballplayers who were outstanding individuals, who had one thing in mind—and that was to beat the hell out of the other clubs we played against. The year we went to Japan we played against a Japanese team and beat them twenty-one games in a row. Nobody else had done that. Stengel said, "Don't let them beat you," and so we just gave them the works.

Baseball has been good to me. I made a good salary and I have worked for some fine people. Dan Topping and Del Webb were outstanding owners, and Mr. Steinbrenner once offered me an executive vice-presidency in the Yankee organization, but it never happened.

The black ballplayer has meant a lot to baseball. You look at the standings and you'll see that all the top hitters are black men. I think the National League got the jump on the American League simply because of the black players. They signed up more black players than the American League. The older ones are gone, like the Willies and the Aarons and other outstanding ballplayers. The major leagues took a long step forward by giving the black man a chance, and he has made good on it.

Elston Howard died on December 14, 1980 in New York City.

BOB GIBSON

"He'd knock you down just for having bad breath."
Joe Garagiola

"Gibson pitches as though he's double-parked."
Vin Scully

Bob Gibson was a super hurler for the St. Louis Cardinals where he started his major league career. In 1970 he won the Cy Young for the second time in three years. He won twenty or more victories five times, beating a Cardinals' club record he shared with Hall of Famer Jay Hanna "Dizzy" Dean. For Gibson the

World Series has been a special showcase. He won seven straight World Series games for St. Louis. In 1964 he pitched against the Yankees for twenty-seven innings, won two games, lost one, and set a strikeout record of thirty-one for the series. In the 1967 series against the Boston Red Sox, Gibson pitched and won three complete ballgames, giving up a total of three runs and fourteen hits. The fourteen-hit total tied a fall classic mark set in the 1905 Series by New York Giant Christy Mathewson against Connie Mack's Philadelphia Athletes. In 1968, pitching against Detroit, he won the first game on a 4–0 shutout, setting a single series game record for strikeouts with seventeen.

Gibson, who played basketball at Creighton University and with the Harlem Globetrotters, says his proudest memory was the entire 1968 season when he was voted the Most Valuable Player, won twenty-two games, lost nine, struck out 268, had an 1.12 ERA, and won both the MVP and the Cy Young Awards. Of the thirty-four contests he appeared in that year, he says he doesn't believe he pitched one bad game.

Bob Gibson exuded competitiveness, consistency, and talent as he dominated the 1960s and early '70s with his intimidating fastball and disappearing slider. He was 251 and 174 lifetime with a 2.91 ERA over seventeen seasons. He was elected to the Baseball Hall of Fame in 1981.

CLEON JONES

CLEON JONES: I'd like to tell you about some of the things a black ballplayer has to put up with in the major leagues, even if he is a star. First of all, I would like to elaborate about the minor league side of it, because this is where the problem starts. I know when I played in the minors as a young kid, your thing is to play baseball. You're not going out to the park to worry about what the people are going to say or what they think about you. Everybody needs to play in a relaxed atmosphere. When you hear someone shout out of the stands: "No-good nigger" and stuff like that, as a young ballplayer, it kind of inhibits you.

I think the one thing that I related to that helped me when I was young was the fact that Jackie Robinson had done so well under such a tremendous strain. Larry Doby, too. I remember I had just hit a home run in the minor leagues and I walked into the batter's box and a fellow hollered out of the stands, "Hey nigger, if you hit another home run we're coming down there to get you." I looked around to see where it was coming from. The guy stood up and said, "Yeah, I'm talking to you!" This was in the Carolina League. Again, you related to Jackie Robinson and all the things he went through. He had so many people against him, but he did it. He came through it. I think that Jackie Robinson was one of the greatest individuals that ever lived, not just talent-wise, but in every respect. He had a job to do and he did it.

In the major leagues I think things are a little different, because you are able to associate a lot more because you have a lot more black ballplayers on your club. You can relate to them and you kind of help one another out. There are many things in the game that need improving. For instance, then as a black ballplayer when things happened, a white manager in many cases had a black coach talking to you instead of talking to you himself. The guys didn't like that. A man is a man—you'd like to forget about this color thing. Hank Aaron once elaborated about the fact that the Braves wanted to have a Black Day on which black people would come out for him to show their appreciation. But he didn't want a totally black situation. He wanted to see people come out, not for a day for Hank Aaron, but because they wanted to do it, regardless.

Now, about this reputation I had for being lazy. In fact, several black ballplayers had this reputation. You see, I walked around nonchalantly, and I went out on the field and did the things I thought were necessary. I'm not a holler guy; I'm not a guy who does a lot of flashy things. So they said, hell, he's lazy. They said he doesn't want to work. But I felt when a game was on I did a good job, a better job than anybody. You see, I can relate to it because I'm black. Take Amos Otis, for example. When he was with the Mets he had a tag. They said Amos was lazy because he didn't want to play. They said he didn't want to play in the big leagues. Then he became a star over at Kansas City, and it's because they didn't understand.

The whites didn't understand the blacks and they didn't care to get into it. They say this is the way with blacks, let's accept it and go along with it. It was just an unfortunate situation. Hank Aaron at first was tagged a lazy ballplayer because he did everything with ease, but he did it so well no one could say he was lazy because he really did a job. When you have good days, no one can tag you one way or the other.

As for total integration, it has not yet taken place in the major leagues. When you sit on a plane, blacks sit together. If you're a Spanish ballplayer, you sit with the other Spanish ballplayers. This is the way they have the seating arrangements. All the blacks sit together. Nobody cares who they room with as long as they are compatible. I don't care who I room with. I wouldn't have minded rooming with a white ballplayer. A man is a man.

In 1976 I was asked why there weren't more black pitchers and infielders in the bigs. Well, I think when a black ballplayer gets into the major leagues, if he doesn't get off to a tremendous start, he has so many other things going for him, like he might be able to run and hit, then they'll say, hey, why waste time with this guy as a pitcher, he might not develop anyway, so let's put him in the outfield, or let's put him some other place. They just don't want to take the time they take with a white player because they get so much more money. If a white ballplayer has any potential he gets pretty good cash for signing so they have to take time to develop him. You have a black guy who wants to play and in all probability needs every penny you give him and you tell him you can only give him a certain amount. He takes it because he wants to play ball anyway. He has no choice. He wants a chance to play, so he'll sign for X amount of dollars. Then he goes out, and if he doesn't produce and because he doesn't have that big bundle of money, they say let's get rid of him.

TOMMY DAVIS

Baltimore Oriole Tommy Davis came from Brooklyn's Boys High School, where he was the star of a brilliant basketball squad. Along with classmate Lenny Wilkens, Davis turned down college basketball offers to play baseball. In 1959, three years after he finished high school, Davis was a member of the Los Angeles Dodgers. He led the National League in hitting in 1962 and 1963. He was fantastic in the clutch and fielded brilliantly.

In 1965 a broken ankle, followed by a variety of leg ailments, cut his mobility and his playing time. After that, Davis moved to seven different ballclubs in six years: the Mets, the White Sox, Seattle, Houston, the Cubs, Oakland, back to the Cubs, and then to Baltimore. Davis was dropped by Baltimore at the age of thirty-three. At the end of 1972 his legs seemed finished, and so did his career.

By 1973 the designated-hitter rule came about, and Davis really excelled. He finished the season with a .306 batting average. The best among full-time designated hitters and the third highest among all American League hitters with more than 450 times at bat, Davis drove in 89 runs for the Orioles, his highest total since 1962, when he drove in 153 runs. He never dreamed his legs would go before his bat. The designated-hitter rule rescued Davis from baseball oblivion.

ROD CAREW

Minnesota Twin Rod Carew entered the 1974 season with a .316 career average, tops in the American League, and second in the majors only to Atlanta's Ralph Garr, who had a .318 mark. At the time, only six players—Ty Cobb, Nap Lajoie, Harry Heilmann, Ted Williams, Carl Yastrzemski, teammates Tony Oliva and Carew—had won three or more American League batting crowns. Only Cobb won three in a row.

"The best hitter in the majors."
Sporting News, St. Louis

"Trying to sneak a pitch past him is like trying to sneak the sunrise past the rooster."
Catfish Hunter

"Advising Rod Carew on hitting would be like an art student advising Michaelangelo on painting."
Gene Mauch

In 1970 Carew was off to his best start with a .375 average, but he suffered a knee injury and played only fifty-one games, thus depriving himself of the opportunity to win batting title number four at that time. In winning his third batting crown in 1973 (the others were in 1969 and 1972), Carew batted .350, the highest American League average since 1961, when Detroit's Norm Cash hit .361. Carew captured the 1974 batting championship by hitting .318, the first American Leaguer to win the title three years in a row since Ty Cobb (1917 to 1919).

By the age of twenty-eight, Carew was in the prime of his career. He had experience, maturity, speed, everything. He had been an All-Star selection since his rookie year in 1967 and had been constantly compared to the game's most recent .400 hitter, Red Sox's Ted Williams. Williams has said of Carew, "He's got that great inside-out swing that makes it impossible to fool him." Years ago, Calvin Griffith, Minnesota Twins' president, once said of Carew, "Carew has to be one of the greatest hitters in the history of the game. There have been many great hitters in our league—Cobb, Williams, Heilmann, Tris Speaker, Eddie Collins—yet Carew could pass most of their records. He's that good, he knows how to handle the bat, and he has a great asset in his speed. He's a sure Hall of Famer; he's a true superstar. He's the guy on our club who plays most consistently, day after day. He is our leader." Harmon Killebrew once said, "If he fails to get a hit in one or two games, he can bunt once or twice in the next game for a hit, and beat out a grounder with his great speed."

Carew was the master of legerdemain with the bat. He poked, he punched, and bunted his way to 3,053 hits. His ownership of seven batting titles is surpassed only by Ty Cobb and Honus Wagner and equaled only by Rogers Hornsby and Stan Musial. He used a variety of relaxed and crouched batting stances to hit over .300 for fifteen consecutive seasons with the Twins and the Angels for a lifetime average of .328. He was honored as the American League's Rookie of the Year in 1967 and the American League's MVP ten years later. Carew was named to an incredible seventeen straight All-Star teams. He entered the Hall of Fame in 1991. But even as a Hall of Famer, Carew is an underrated player whose skills were never fully appreciated by the press.

ROD CAREW: There is more room to hit the ball inside the fences than beyond them. Going into the last month of the 1968 season I was batting .310, but I started going for the fences. I was jerking my head when I swung, and by swinging too hard I finished with a .273 average. The following year Billy Martin told me, "Just hit the ball someplace and get on base, steal bases and score runs . . . that's your job!" From that day on, I never thought about hitting home runs. If a home run develops, that's okay with me. But I don't alter my swing to hit one. Any time that I find myself jerking my head, I take an extra round of batting practice, maybe twice a week.

I disciplined myself to know what I could do with the bat. I knew who I was and I knew who I was not. It's not a shame to go to the opposite field. It's not a shame to lay one down. Unlike most major leaguers who have one batting stance, I had four that varied, depending on the pitcher. One is a square stance with my legs closed. This is good against a good right-handed curve-ball pitcher like Catfish Hunter. Two is a partially open stance with my right foot slightly back. Three, a wide-open stance with my right foot so far back I'm actually facing the pitcher and four, an open stance with me crouched and leaning back, which was good against Nolan Ryan or anybody with good hard stuff. With some pitchers I would change the stance depending on the count or the situation. I could wait as late as when he would bring his hands above his head. I fouled off pitches I didn't like but I thought might be called strikes. Wrist hitters can still get the bat on the ball at the last moment. I've taken the ball out of the catcher's glove sometimes.

In spite of all the discussions about my different batting stances, the different ways I tried to attack the ball, and how I tried to adjust from being a power hitter to a consistent base hitter, I feel that the press has never really given me credit for the all-around way I played the game.

I received credit for hitting .350 or .360 during my career, but I think that my most important contributions were not the homers themselves but my all-around hustle and style of play. I covered the field. I adjusted to the situation at the plate. I bunted to get on base whenever I had to. I went out there and stole extra bases to get myself in scoring position. But most important, I played what I like to call the "middle game." I moved the runners over and made the defense adjust by taking their fielders out of position. I was also a defensive player myself and covered my position because to me that's what baseball is all about.

There are the Reggie Jacksons and the Don Baylors; the sluggers who become the great home-run hitters who any day can hit out of the park. A team always needs power hitters like these. But an all-around first-division ball club also needs aggressive heads-up guys who can consistently set up the RBI situation to tie a ball game up and send it into extra innings where the power hitters can put them ahead.

I've been a solid fielder, playing both first and second bases very defensively and set up the critical double plays that shut down late-inning rallies. I kept a lot of balls from getting out of the infield and turning into base hits, and I kept a lot of runners on base by checking off the steal. You don't see many people talking about fielding at this level because it's considered routine. But when there's lapse in fielding, it always shows up in the final score.

Some of the biggest things I achieved in the major leagues were my seven steals of home plate. Billy Martin taught me the art of stealing home. He explained to me once that the whole secret of "Billyball" was the magic of moving runners over by any means possible, always connecting with the ball, always making the defense guess, and keeping the game exciting for the fans. Fighting for extra bases and stealing home was Billy's way of making the fielding team worry every time a runner got on base. It was one more thing they had to think about. Martin and I worked on the art of stealing home in spring training every season because, as he once said, "Some days you know the hitters might not be hitting. So we're going to work on something to see if we can steal some runs."

Billy Martin practiced with me on timing the pitchers' movements: clocking the wind-up from third base, getting the good short lead off the bag, and breaking for home just when the pitcher was getting ready to deliver. We worked up a sign with our hitters. They knew that once I flashed that sign, they were not supposed to swing. Instead, they were supposed to try to block the catcher out for me so that I could slide under his tag safely. I did it seven consecutive times.

The eighth time I tried to steal home plate was in Seattle. I broke for home like a runaway train and knocked both the catcher and the umpire clean over on their backsides. But the ball was under the catcher. Umpire John Rice got up and called me out, but Billy Martin had seen the whole thing and ran out onto the field as if he were going to tear the stadium apart because he knew I was safe. He'd seen the entire play, knew that the catcher never made the tag, and realized that I had actually gone ahead and broken the record for stealing home. But nobody else saw it. Therefore, as it turned out I only tied the record and that's what went into the books.

I started playing sandlot baseball in the shadow of Yankee Stadium when I was a teenager. A few scouts passing by looking for local talent saw me play and sent my name up to some of the major league organizations. I eventually received offers from about six or seven different teams. I decided to sign with the Minnesota Twins because they were a new club that offered more opportunities for me. I believed I would have been able to make it to the big leagues a lot quicker with the Twins than I would have with the Tigers, with Boston, or with the Chicago White Sox. I was right.

My career began with a bang because I held fast to what I believed in. But my days as a player ended on a note of silence. I had been hoping to return as a player in my twentieth season and probably retire after 1986. Unfortunately, in 1986 no one seemed to be interested in signing me. Maybe my contract was too expensive and the owners truly couldn't afford it. Maybe there was actual collusion among the owners who had gotten together to show younger players that they weren't going to meet my contract demands. Sometimes, I think that some of the owners decided to send a message to the younger players that "we know who Rod Carew is and we're going to work to get players' salaries down." Although I believed that the club owners were working with each other to keep me out of baseball, there was nothing I could do about it.

Eventually I consoled myself that if no one called to pick up my contract, I'd still spent nineteen good years in the big leagues. No amount of collusion would take that away. I had no real regrets, and my forced retirement would give me a chance to be with my wife and my three daughters. Therefore even before it was all over I had decided that I wasn't going back to baseball. In the end I did get a call from the San Francisco Giants, but because I'd made the decision to retire, I stuck with it. And that was how my active playing career ended.

Rod Carew was elected to the Baseball Hall of Fame in 1991.

MAURY WILLS

Maury Wills became a legend in 1962 when he broke Ty Cobb's 1915 record for the total number of bases stolen in a single season. Like Henry Aaron, Maury was an aggressive black ballplayer making an assault on another legendary performance that had remained untouched for over forty years. Also like Henry Aaron, Maury was breaking a record which was established at a time when black athletes were not allowed to compete in the major leagues. Maury not only broke Cobb's record convincingly, he also changed the way the game of baseball was played by demonstrating precisely what fearless base-running could accomplish.

Before Wills, most team managers looked upon stolen bases as good or bad fortune depending upon who stole the base. However, Maury showed that stolen bases could become part of a game-winning strategy, especially when a manager didn't have a "murderer's row" in his lineup. Maury inspired the Dodger teams of the early sixties with his aggressive stealing. He intimidated opposing infielders, pitchers, and catchers alike. He showed that a team with solid pitching and a good defense need only score three or so runs in a game to win. Maury also showed that with a fearless base-stealing strategy, runners could move themselves into scoring position without waiting for a slugger at the plate to bang them home. People watched Maury very carefully, especially the young Billy Martin who would one day incorporate much of Maury's aggression and heads-up base running into what would eventually be called "Billyball."

Maury also became one of the elite group of four black ballplayers to become team managers. In a sport where so many black players have given their all for their teams, it is a disgrace that there aren't more black managers. But Maury showed that he could make the transition from player to manager and contribute to a younger generation of players. Maury still teaches his baserunning skills today, almost thirty years after he broke Ty Cobb's record.

MAURY WILLS: As I approached the stolen base record set by Ty Cobb back in 1915, I didn't even realize there was a record. Cobb had ninety-six bases and his count stood for over forty years. I broke it when I stole 104 bases, and I did without having to put up with the racial attacks that Henry Aaron had to face when he approached Ruth's home run mark. As for me, I just kind of sneaked up on Cobb without a lot of fanfare and no one realized it.

I stole bases out of downright necessity. Someone had to get in scoring position, and on the Dodgers at that time we didn't have a lot of power hitting. Therefore, you had to go after whatever bases you could get: you bunt, you walk, you squeeze out a bouncer past the shortstop. But once you're standing on first, you know your lineup doesn't have the power to move you around. You're stuck unless you put yourself in scoring position. Our Dodger teams had great speed and great pitching. They also played a good defensive game and could contain the other team's batters. Therefore, if we got three or so runs, we knew that was all we were going to get from our hitting. But it was OK because with our great pitching, it was all we needed if we could move our base runners around. That's what I did. I got into position by stealing second or third so that I could be moved across the plate by a single or a sacrifice fly. The strategy worked because it turned a two-run performance by our team into a three- or four-run game. Once we were a couple of runs up, our pitching and fielding did the rest.

It was July, 1962 and I was close to having stolen eighty bases, and some sports writer began talking about an old Ty Cobb record that was ninety-six bases. On the way up to number ninety-six, I broke a record of eighty some-odd bases held by Bob Bescher in Cincinnati. Then as I got closer to ninety, people started to talk about Cobb's mark. By the time I had reached ninety-two, I realized there was a real goal that I would achieve. But no one really perceived it in the same way they saw Aaron's approach to Babe Ruth's record because my stolen bases were in the larger context of just moving runners around.

When I would steal a base, it wouldn't stop a game the way a home run did with its all its drama as the fans followed the ball's arc into the stands. Home runs begin with a loud crack at the plate that echoes over the whole field. People ooh and ah. The time it takes for the ball to travel allows fans and players to stand around and watch the batter turn third and head for home to get his congratulations. When you steal a base, it's different. You time the pitcher, make your break, and slide into the bag in a cloud of dust.

Everybody's watching the ball, not you. It happens so fast that by the time the umpire gives the sign, the game has already started moving again and the pitcher is winding up to put the batter out to make up for the base he just lost. The batter swings and people forget about you.

You do take a physical beating when you steal a base. You get knocked around and receive a lot of bruises and cuts from the way the basemen slap that hardball down on you as hard as they can. They're out to tag the hell out of you because they want you to know that you've been tagged and the ump to see it through the flying dirt in order to call it. But a baseman also wants to intimidate the runner by beating him up if he tries to steal a base. When I would try for home, catchers would never tag me properly or gently. They tried to make me eat the ball.

Because stealing bases is ninety percent psychological, you have to eliminate all fear of failing from your mind. When I teach base running and stealing for the Dodger organization, I demonstrate how far to lead off the bag, how to watch the pitcher's wind-up, how to time the catcher, and how to gauge distance. Those are the fundamentals that take me ten minutes to illustrate. All the rest of the time I teach new players to overcome the fear of failing in public, the fear of the tag. I tell them it's better getting picked off at first base by being too aggressive than to get picked off at second because you weren't aggressive enough or you were too afraid. I commiserate with new players. I understand that it's tough when you have 60,000 fans watching you from the stands and another few million people watching on TV. I tell a player that when he makes his break, the camera zooms in and the whole world is watching the runner and the throw. I tell that player to go after that bag as if no one else is there except the second baseman and the ball. Forget about failing, I tell them, just go after that bag.

I once said in my own book that had it not been for my record of 104 bases in 1962, there would not have been a Lou

Brock or a Vince Coleman. There would have not been a Rickie Henderson either. They had a chance to play baseball in a different way because of the bases I stole. After the other teams saw what the Dodgers were doing in 1962—deception, quickness, heads-up running—they opened their spring training camps by teaching all their speedsters the art of base stealing.

By 1963, I could see a deliberate strategic change in the way ball clubs approached the art of base running because coaches saw that when they moved runners around by stealing bases, it was not a fluke of luck. A runner could get that extra base and even start a rally because he wasn't afraid to challenge a pitcher or a catcher. A team could earn extra runs because first, they put people in scoring position more times than if they relied only on power at the plate and second, because they were able to shake up the pitcher's concentration.

Good base running also helps the batter because it gives the pitcher something else to worry about when he's staring down at the plate trying to look intimidating. I don't like to claim that Maury Wills revolutionized the game of baseball. But I do believe that managers saw what I could do and built it into their strategies. Once it was proven that base-stealing was a strong offensive weapon, other teams started doing it.

In August, 1988, I was appointed manager of the Seattle Mariners, the third black manager in baseball. It was rewarding. I had wanted to manage for years and had even tried to become a player-manager. But that didn't happen after my playing career had ended. So in order to stay in uniform, I went to Mexico to manage because major league teams kept saying that I didn't have any managerial experience. It was the same black thing all over again. Blacks can play, but they can't manage. GMs also wanted me to go to the minor leagues, but I didn't want to do that. It was too low a level for me. Other managers who came off the playing field didn't have to go to the minors to get their start, so why should I?

I went to Mexico and managed teams down there where I spent my time bouncing along these twenty-two-hour bus trips on those little winding roads to get to the games. That really rattled my teeth, but it didn't matter because I wanted to stay in uniform. I was also a little bitter because I knew that most of the managers on the teams where I had taught base-running in the past didn't want me around because they knew that I aspired to manage. It was a tough thing to accept that I could teach a skill well, but that what I really wanted to do was a threat to the people I worked for. So the managers utilized me to for what I could do but didn't want me there. They got rid of me as soon as they could, and I accepted that. I was a threat to their jobs as long as I wanted to manage. I wanted my own job, though, so I found myself placating them and subordinating my own personal dignity just to stay in uniform. It took a lot out of me.

Then Ed O'Brien of the Mariners called me in August 1988 and asked me if I could manage. "You bet," I told him, and I was hired right away. I knew it was a great opportunity that I'd been looking forward to for years. After all the changes I helped to instill in the game, I knew I had prepared myself to manage. But it wasn't a very good time for me because I had gotten myself into a relationship with alcohol that I knew would ultimately interfere with my life. I needed outside help in order to deal with my problems. Baseball had been my only real relationship while I was playing. Yet after I had stopped playing, I sensed something was missing and jumped right into what would have to be called a "toxic" relationship that was stronger than I was. Because I tend to bull things through, however, I vowed to take my drinking problems head on and lick them all by myself. But the harder I tried, the deeper in I slid. And this is when I got the opportunity to manage. Unfortunately, by the time it was over, everything had just slipped clean away.

In retrospect, I honestly feel that none of the problems I faced as a new manager in Seattle had anything to do with my being black. Ed O'Brien hired me and I did not run into one area where I felt that being black had to do with my demise as a manager. I take responsibility for my own actions. I know that many people thought that race was one of the problems. People said that I was an easy scapegoat to take the blame for the Mariners because I was a black manager at a weak ball club. But that wasn't the case.

When I started I felt that if I could just show some improvement in the team's performance then I would be doing OK. I didn't think that they wanted me to demonstrate that I could change things overnight. I assumed that the management knew it was going to take some time to gradually build the team, and therefore I didn't feel the pressure to shake things up. But I have to take the ultimate responsibility for my being fired. It was all my fault because I was not able to deal with my personal problems.

I played fourteen seasons from 1959 to 1972 in Los Angeles, Montreal, and Pittsburgh, and I have a very positive view of the way things have changed for the black ballplayer since 1947. I disagree with what a lot of other black players have said about the lack of improved conditions in the majors. Back in 1947 for example, you didn't see black players just sitting on the bench. The black player had to be good enough to start and play every day whether he was hurting or not. No bones sticking out of his flesh or anything would keep him from running onto the field. If a black player was on your team you played him. Now that's changed in the past ten years because you have utility players who are black that you can keep in reserve. Today you also have specialty players who are black and DHs whom you can use in specific situations. That's one of the big changes from thirty years ago.

You also see journeyman black ballplayers today that you never saw thirty years ago because back then if you were black, you were great or you weren't on the team. A Jackie Robinson had to be a potential superstar to make a lineup. Today, one sees black players who will take a few years to reach their full potential. Owners are willing to wait for them to blossom. Teams are giving younger black players a chance to prove themselves. There's a lot of pressure on black rookies to perform, but less so than years ago. There is an offsetting factor, though. The young black ballplayer today has to be better than the comparable white ballplayer he'll come up against in order to make the roster in the first place. So things are not completely equal. Just to get selected, a black has to be a potentially excellent player.

RICHIE ALLEN

Despite big salaries and good treatment in the clubhouse, blacks still have humiliations to cope with, as they had in the 1960s when Richie Allen first came up. A simple thing like getting a haircut in spring training might have required a few hours' travel for black ballplayers. In some cities black outfielders still often have to close their ears to racial obscenities and be wary of flying objects when they range too close to the fans when pulling down fly balls. Any time a black player asserts himself he earns the reputation of being hard to handle because of his supposed special sensitivity to racial abuse. And if outspoken black ballplayers assert themselves on the issue of money as have Dave Winfield, Reggie Jackson, and Darryl Strawberry, the criticism is especially intense.

A case in point is Richie Allen, once the major leagues' stormy petrel, who was anything but the white man's idea of the black athlete. Allen was the equal of most white ballplayers in his independent attitude, his reckless off-the-field escapades, and his own skills. Richie Allen was the first black player to play minor league baseball in Little Rock. There he got the treatment:

"Nigger go home" signs on his car windshield, obscene phone calls, and death threats. No decent restaurant in Little Rock would serve him. He lived through it all and at the age of twenty-one joined the Philadelphia Phillies. Allen batted .318 his first full year and led the league in runs scored.

When his teammates were working themselves into condition in spring training, Allen at the time could be found in Florida at a race track. He kept on hitting .300 and more, and in 1966 he hit forty homers. The Philly fans gave him a hard time anyway because he was black and did his own thing. It is true that there have been white ballplayers who have been subjected to mistreatment from the fans—Ted Williams is a case in point—but all of their abuse combined did not match that which was inflicted upon Allen by the Philly patrons.

Allen eventually had to take to wearing a batting helmet to protect himself from being hit by missiles from the stands. He asked to be traded and subsequently wound up with St. Louis. After thirty-four home runs and 101 runs batted in, the Cardinals shipped him off to the Dodgers. Allen presented a morale problem in Los Angeles and he was shipped to the Chicago White Sox where he led the league in home runs (thirty-seven) and runs batted in (113) and finished third in the batting averages. Chuck Tanner, Allen's manager in the windy city, said Allen would spend a lifetime with the club. He said he would go right from the White Sox to the Hall of Fame. "One thing is for sure," said Tanner. "Allen will never go back to Philadelphia."

But Tanner was wrong. Two weeks before of the end of the American League campaign, Richie Allen abruptly retired. However, he ended his "retirement" when he went back to the Phillies. From there he went to the Oakland A's where he completed his career in 1971. By the time he finally retired for good, he had hit 351 home runs.

THE HEAVY HITTERS

REGGIE JACKSON

By the time he was twenty-eight Reggie Jackson had already reached his prime and baseball fans could see that playing baseball was what he did better than any other player in the American League. When the 1973 regular season ended, for example, Reggie Jackson led his league in five offensive categories: home runs (thirty-two), RBIs (117), runs scored (ninety-nine), game-winning hits (eighteen), and slugging percentage, the production of extra base hits (.531). He also hit .293, the tenth-best American League average. On the basepaths he was daring, diving into bases à la Pepper Martin, stretching singles into doubles and doubles into triples.

At one time he was somewhat maladroit, defensively. But ultimately right-fielder Reggie Jackson made a habit of Ringling Brothers catches and bullet-like pegs to the infield and home plate. In the 1973 Series Jackson kicked the hell out of the New York Mets and helped the A's with his hitting and spectacular outfield defense. He received the league's and the Series' MVP.

From 1976 to 1987, Reggie reigned supreme on the Baltimore Orioles, the Yankees, the California Angels, and again on the A's in his final major league season. Reggie put himself in the World Series record book with some outstanding feats in 1977, earning himself the moniker "Mr. October." His five home runs set a series record; so did his three consecutive homers in a single game, his four homers in four consecutive official at-bats over two games, his twenty-five total base hits, and his ten runs scored. His three homers tied the one-game series record established by the Babe in 1928. As of this writing, Reggie is a coach with the Oakland A's.

At 6 feet and 200 pounds, he was built like a bull, and put his 17-inch biceps, 27-inch thighs, and 36-ounce bat to good use. In 1969, his second full year in the majors, Jackson hit forty-seven home runs. A lot of those blows traveled well over 500 feet. He has clouted eight home runs in six days, accounted for ten runs batted in one game, and hit .360 over a seven-game stretch.

When Ted Williams first watched Jackson swing, he said, "He's the most natural hitter I've ever seen." Baseball manager Frank Robinson once said, "Reggie is a smart hitter. This time you may strike him out, but next time he'll be waiting." In fact, Jackson would go to the plate with a plan for every pitcher. "I know what to expect and I know what I want. If I want a fast ball, I move up in the batter's box as though I'm expecting a curve. When the pitcher tries to blow it by me, I'm ready. It's good-by baseball."

One of the main ingredients in Jackson's game was passion to win and to dominate. He once said, "To hit is to show strength. It's two against one at the plate, the pitcher and the catcher versus you. When I'm up there, I'm thinking, 'Try everything you want. Rub up the ball, move your fielders around, try any God damn thing, I'm going to hit the ball.' Man, do I love to hit that little round son of a bitch out of the park and make 'em say 'Wow.'"

Reggie had his fallouts with Yankee management and with Billy Martin over the years. When he was traded back to Oakland at the end of his career, he negotiated a precedent setting agreement in which he was given a percentage of the gate. This was the team's recognition of Reggie's consummate skills not only as a player but as a personality who would bring people to the ball park. Reggie has been criticized for arrogance—most talented black ball players are criticized for arrogance—and for having an "attitude." But Reggie has consistently been quoted as saying that he'll stand up for what he thinks is right and he won't be pushed around.

AL DOWNING

AL DOWNING: A black ballplayer in the major leagues today has, I think, a lot more opportunities. I think that if you can do the job better than the next guy than you have a good chance to win a position. Where it's a little unfair for the black ballplayer is when it comes to the fringe jobs, the reserve jobs. You didn't see too many black ballplayers in the role of utility infielder to the fifth or sixth outfielder. Or say, even a relief pitcher, because these jobs were difficult to get. If you weren't a superstar it was very difficult for the black ballplayer to stay up.

I think in some respects there is still something of a quota system remaining in the major leagues concerning the number of black ballplayers on a team. You look at the major league rosters and you'll discover that each club has about an equal number of blacks so they can have somebody to room with. You would have thought that this kind of thinking would have gone out years ago but it's still there.

Take a ballplayer like Orlando Cepeda who led the league as the designated hitter, but was released because they said he couldn't run and they were going for the youth movement. Yet they were in the thick of the pennant race. They definitely could have used his bat at that time. And I'm sure if he were white they would not have cut him. Isn't it curious that outstanding black players like Reggie Smith and Orlando Cepeda were both cut from the Boston roster despite single contributions they were making at the time of their dismissal?

I first came to the major leagues in 1961 and had a very pleasant career. I've been with two of the great organizations in the history of baseball, the Yankees in the early sixties and then the Dodgers. And I've been very fortunate that I've been on many teams that have been pennant contenders. So I've been with ballplayers who knew how to play the game and not with a lot of Mickey Mouse players. They were there to win. As for the black ballplayer's future, just you think about it.

You hear some guy say, "Yes, you've got to have minor league experience, because it's the best place to learn," and then you look at some of the managers in the big leagues, like a guy like Frank Quilici, who managed the Minnesota Twins. He wasn't a super ballplayer but he had a good knowledge of the game, and they gave him a job just like that. He never had any minor league experience. You don't necessarily need minor league experience. They're using that as an excuse because even though there have been four black managers, just look at all the black ballplayers that are qualified and able to manage but who aren't hired.

There are quite a few of them, all superstar ballplayers. These are men who had to know how to play the whole game before they came to the majors. They had to do everything, and they were taught before they ever got to the big leagues how to play the game. And these guys not only know how to play the game, they know how to run the game. They had experience in managing when they played in the black leagues. When it comes to managerial and executive positions for the blacks in the majors, racism still exists.

LOU BROCK

BROCK BREAKS RECORD

"Lou Brock stole second base in the seventh inning of the Cardinals' game against the Philadelphia Phillies tonight and set a major league record of 105 stolen bases for one season. Overall he stole 118 bases for that year. (Rickey Henderson set the current major league record when he stole 130 bases in 1982 with the Oakland A's.) Brock's theft, his second of the game, came during the Cards' 142nd game and his 134th. It eclipsed the previous record of 104 set by the Los Angeles Dodgers' Maury Wills in 1962.

His first steal came in the opening inning following a single to left before an enthusiastic Busch Stadium crowd of 27,285. Brock led off the seventh with a single to left. Following the steal, Brock's teammates and photographers poured onto the field and Brock was presented with the historic base that he stole.

The game was stopped and Brock, who addressed the crowd, embraced the Cards' second baseman, Ted Sizemore, an injured player who usually bats behind him. In a salute to his throng of admirers, the 35-year-old outfielder said, 'The left-field fans probably knew I was going to steal 105 before I did. They were behind me all the way.'"

Associated Press, St. Louis, Sept. 10, 1974

Brock was not only one of the most prolific base stealers in baseball (938 lifetime), but also one of the best clutch hitters in history. In the 1964 World Series against the Yankees he hit a solid, dependable .300; in the 1967 Series against Boston he hit a whopping .414, and in the 1968 "fall classic" against Detroit he surpassed himself by belting an astounding .464. Lou Brock was inducted into the Hall of Fame in 1985.

LOU BROCK: I would say the turning point in my baseball career, if you could call it a turning point, was the moment that I really arrived as a big-league ballplayer, in Chicago, playing against Cincinnati one day. I went up in the vines at Wrigley Field and came down with a spectacular catch. The moment I made that catch and came down, it seemed as if the whole world was lifted off my shoulders . . . from that particular moment I knew my way around. I knew what I had to do in order to compete. Everything became clear to me at that point. Somewhere in every guy's career that happens to him.

I always wanted to play baseball. I suppose nearly every kid, from the age of ten on, has thoughts of playing ball. You do dream about it. I think once you leave high school that dream sort of falls away and you begin to think of other interesting things you want to do in life. Of course, I went to Southern University, and at that time I was more interested in an education than a professional sports career. But things might happen in your life that turn you toward the big league.

My first introduction to baseball was somewhere around the age of nine or ten. Being one of the mischievous kids, I recall hitting my teacher with a spitball. I was punished for it. The punishment was to go to the library and then to stand before the class and give a report on five baseball players, black and white: Stan Musial, Jackie Robinson, Roy Campanella, Don Newcombe, and Joe DiMaggio. I knew nothing about these guys at the time, and after doing some research the one thing that struck me and sort of caught my attention was the fact that they got an awful lot for meal money. Money just for eating! That was one of the aspects of baseball that caught my fancy at the age of ten.

After I broke Maury Wills's record, a lot of people have asked me what was involved in base stealing. First of all, you've got to be able to hit. But the make-up of stealing bases is more than meets the eye. People generally refer to the myth that speed has a lot to do with it, but I recall at a much younger age having as much speed as anybody in baseball. Now there are more than thirty-five guys who could run much faster than I did. But one factor is experience, the other is being able to react and how do you react. There are a lot of mechanics that one has to go through, and a lot of time and effort have to be put into it. What I did was a repetition of things I'd learned over the years. But the most important part of learning is how to take off. People saw Bob Hayes run in 9.1. If you look at Bob Hayes getting out of the block you would swear he couldn't do a 9.1.

There have been guys who were able to get out of the blocks much faster but could not maintain or sustain. The key to stealing bases is getting the jump on thrusting one's body. Thrusting your body in motion—having that good breakaway. If you have that good thrust or breakaway, in my opinion, in a ninety-foot distance span, then speed is not that important. Although it is important, it is not the key factor at that moment. Plus you've got to have that mental positive thought about going down there to the next base. As Maury Wills said, "You cannot be afraid of being thrown out."

You actually steal on the pitcher. It's a time element. I think that any time you can go from first base to second base using a good breakaway, reading the keys properly, and if you can run down there in a 3.1 or 3.2, chances are you are going to be called safe. Every time you go down in 3.4 or 3.5, you will be out. You're working in a time span, and this is why the breakaway means so much. This is why getting out of the block is so important. You put each pitcher into a category and study it and take it from there.

There are certain pitchers who were tough to steal on. There were certain styles that I hated, like Don Sutton, Andy Messersmith, and Jim Barr. These pitchers decreased the margin of error because of their quickness, not their velocity on the ball, but their body movement. I've always said that each one of these guys could deliver a baseball, release a baseball, inside of six-tenths of a second, and based on that alone, it didn't give a base runner much time under that 3.2 category which I mentioned earlier. But there were guys who released a ball in about eight-tenths of a second. That's about the average, and those were the guys I could steal on.

What do I love about baseball? I love the psychological warfare of the game. And I feel that we blacks have the capacity to do anything the average white player can do, namely manager work or work in the front office. However, the system just doesn't allow us to do it. My contention is that sports is the only industry that has allowed the black to come in and compete under the same rules. Other aspects of American society see the rules changing once you take the uniform off, and until we are able to wipe out some of those things through political moves and people moves, only then will we have the right to participate and do what we want to do from a business and economic point of view. Professionally speaking, as long as the rules remain the same, we are going to be at the top, because they only choose the better black ballplayers. I still think there is a quota system in sports, especially in baseball.

The greatest ballplayer I ever saw since I was in the bigs? I would say Chicago's Billy Williams: He's just a guy who could do everything. Best hitter I ever saw is Billy Williams. Just one great all-around ballplayer. I loved the way the guy played and I admired his attitude. If I had ever tried to emulate anybody in the majors, it would be Billy Williams, who is now a coach.

BILLY WILLIAMS

He was not a very colorful performer, but the soft-spoken Chicago Cub with the classic swing hit a rock-ribbed .290 with 426 home runs over eighteen campaigns. He was National League Rookie of the Year in 1961, won a batting title with .333 in 1972, and held the National League mark for consecutive games played (1,117) until this record was broken by Steve Garvey.

"The foremost Cub with the sweet swing, the cool and calm attitude, the great wrist action and all the other important requisites required of a batting champion."
Sporting News, April 27, 1963

"I'm just a ballplayer, a loner, trying to win everyday."
Billy Williams

Billy Williams was born on June 15, 1938 in Whistler, Alabama, three miles out of Mobile. He was the fifth and last child of Frank and Jessie Mary Williams. Williams started playing baseball in grammar school. By the time he was in high school he had come to the attention of several major league scouts. He was signed up in the Cub organization by scout Ivy Griffin.

In 1956 and 1957 he played with Ponca City. There he showed immediate signs of his tremendous batting ability. Four years later, in 1961 after two brief "cups of coffee" with the Cubs in 1959 and 1960, Williams played his first full major league season. He was named the 1961 National League Rookie of the Year—hitting .278 with twenty-five homers and eighty-six runs batted in.

From September 22, 1963 to September 3, 1970, Williams never missed a game—1,117 consecutive contests. Only two other players in the history of baseball ever played more games in succession—Henry Louis Gehrig, the "Iron Horse" of the Yankees (2,130) and another one-time Yankee, Everitt Deacon Scott, with 1,307.

On October 3, 1974, the Oakland A's acquired the thirty-six-year-old Billy Williams in exchange for reliever Harold Knowles, Bob Locker, and infielder Manny Trillo. At the time, A's owner Charley Finley said, "We feel that he will be the first designated hitter in the American League. He hits with authority and consistency, as evidenced by his outstanding record." Billy Williams was elected to the Baseball Hall of Fame in 1987.

HENRY "HANK" AARON

It all started April 23, 1954. Hank Aaron hit his first major league homer off Vic Raschi of the St. Louis Cardinals. On Monday evening, April 8, 1974, Henry Aaron ended the great pursuit and passed George Herman "Babe" Ruth as the leading home-run hitter in baseball history when he hit number 715 before a national television audience and 53,775 on hand in Atlanta Stadium.

AARON HITS 714, TIES THE BABE
New York Daily News, headline, April 5, 1974

AARON BLASTS 715th HOMER IN ATLANTA AND BREAKS RUTH'S RECORD
The New York Times, headline, April 9, 1974

*Jesus Christ! I'm sitting in front of my TV set and Hank
Aaron has just broken Babe Ruth's home-run record. As the
tears of joy stream from my eyes, I know that this has to be my
ultimate sports thrill . . . and that's saying a lot. I was sitting in
section 22 at the Polo Grounds when Bobby Thomson hit it out
against the Dodgers; I was at the Yankee Stadium for Don
Larson's perfect game in the World Series; thrilled to many
great Sugar Ray Robinson performances; went ecstatic over
Jimmy Brown's scoring three touchdowns against the Giants at
the Yankee Stadium in 1963. But this home run by Aaron has to
be the tops!*

"In that great crowd around home plate, I found him
looking over his mother's shoulder, hugging her to him,
and suddenly I saw what many people have never been
able to see in him: deep emotion. I'd never seen that
before. He had such cool. He never gets excited. He's
so stable. And I look, and he had tears hanging on his
lids. I could hardly believe it. 'However, here it is,' I said.
I put the ball in his hand. He said, 'Thanks, kid,' and
touched me on the shoulder. I kept staring at him and it
was then that it was brought home to me what his home
run meant, not only to him, but to all of us."

Tom House

The forty-year-old Atlanta Braves' outfielder broke the
record on his second swing of a noisy evening. It was a soaring
line drive in the fourth inning off lefty Al Downing of the Los
Angeles Dodgers. It cleared the fence in left center field, some
385 feet from home plate. "I have never gone out on a ball field
and given less than my level best. When I hit it tonight, all I
thought about was that I wanted to touch all the bases," he said.

As the man from Mobile jogged around the bases after
hitting his 715th major league home run, in a career that began

twenty-five years ago with the Indianapolis Clowns in the old Negro leagues, a skyrocket arched over the jammed stadium. It was seven minutes after nine o'clock, some thirty-nine years after Ruth had hit his 714th and four days after Aaron hit his 714th on his first swing of the bat in the season's opener.

Henry was born on February 5th 1934, the third of eight children born to Herbert and Estelle Aaron. In his grammar-school days, Aaron was a catcher for one of the clubs in the Louisiana Recreation League. When he entered Central High School he had to play softball, since the school could not afford equipment for a hardball team. He played shortstop, third base, and catcher for the softball team, and he was an outstanding footballer as a halfback and end. After two years at Central he transferred to Allen Institute, a private school in Mobile. It wasn't until his junior year in high school that Aaron got his first chance to play ball on a semi-pro level. Henry played for the Mobile Black Bears, and on the final Sunday of the season the Bears met the Indianapolis Clowns. The Clowns were so impressed with Aaron's's performance that they offered him $200 a month to play for them the following year. Aaron led the Negro American League his first season with the Clowns by hitting .467. Strangely enough, Aaron was batting cross-handed at the time, a habit he corrected long before he came up to the majors. After watching Aaron play a Negro league game in 1952, Milwaukee Braves scout Dewey Griggs recommended Aaron to the Braves' general manager, John Quinn. The Braves then purchased Aaron for $2,500 down and $7,500 later.

In 1952 he played with the Braves' farm club at Eau Claire in the Northern League. In eighty-seven games he hit .336, which was good enough to earn him Rookie of the Year and a place on the All-Star team. In 1953 Aaron moved up to Jacksonville in the Class-A Sally League. He literally tore apart the South Atlantic League pitching. He led the league in batting (.362), hits (208), runs (115), and runs batted in (125). He also was second in the league in triples and hit twenty-two home runs. In fielding he topped the league in assists. It is not surprising he was voted the league's Most Valuable Player.

Aaron was a second baseman his one year at Jacksonville, but Milwaukee had a plethora of infield prospects in the organization and put him in the outfield during the off season while he was playing winter ball in the Puerto Rican League. During that winter the Braves purchased outfielder Bobby Thomson from the Giants, and it looked then like another year in the minor leagues for Aaron. But during spring training Bobby Thomson suffered a triple fracture of his right ankle after sliding into second base, and Aaron replaced him in the outfield. Henry hit .280 and drove in sixty-nine runs before he too suffered a broken ankle, that September. He recuperated quickly and the following season he hit .314, with twenty-seven homers and 106 runs batted in.

Aaron won the batting championship in 1956, hitting .328. The Braves, however, lost the flag on the last day of the season. In 1957 Hank led the league in home runs with forty-four, and the Braves won the National League championship. Hank was voted the National League's Most Valuable Player award. It was a great year for Aaron. He hit .322 and drove in 132 runs. One of the highlights of his career happened on the night of September 23rd. The Braves were playing the St. Louis Cardinals. With the score tied in the eleventh inning, Henry came up with one on. He then hit Billy Muffett's fast ball over the center-field fence. His home run won the game and the pennant. At the age of twenty-three, Hank Aaron was already a superstar.

In the World Series against the Yankees, Hank had eleven hits in seven games, batted .393, and led both clubs with three homers and seven runs batted in, helping the Braves beat the Yankees four games to three. The Braves won the flag again in 1958, but this time the Yankees beat them in the fall classic. In 1959 the Braves lost in a playoff with the Dodgers. That year

Aaron won another batting title. He hit .355, the best of his career. He also led the National League with 223 hits and 400 total bases. His thirty-nine home runs and 123 RBIs were also close to the best in the League.

After 1959 the Braves started to disintegrate, but Hank continued to remain a star. In the 1963 season he became only the fifth man in the history of baseball to hit more than thirty home runs and steal more than thirty bases in the same year. Aaron was never a "hot dog." He did things quietly and efficiently. After his tenth season more and more people began to see how great he was and began to compare him to the other recognized superstars at the time, Willie Mays and Mickey Mantle.

By 1966 the Braves migrated to Atlanta. Hank hit forty-four home runs his first year there. Subsequently, that '66 season paid off in his receiving his first $100,000 contract. That year, on April 20th in Philadelphia, he hit home run 400. In 1968 his round-trip total reached 500. Shortly thereafter he passed Mickey Mantle and started gaining on Willie Mays. It was then that people began to realize he had a chance to catch Babe Ruth.

In 1969, in the playoffs against the Mets, Henry hit three home runs in a losing cause. In 1970, he collected his 3,000th base hit. He hit forty-seven home runs in 1971, batted .327, and drove in 118 runs. Before the 1972 campaign Hank signed a new contract with Atlanta. It was for $200,000, making him the highest-paid player in baseball history, and deservedly so.

HANK AARON: When I was playing in the Sally League, I never dreamed that I would break Babe Ruth's record of 714 home runs. I never thought about being in the big leagues, really, so I couldn't have thought about breaking his record. I never looked beyond the Sally League while I was playing there.

I remember the racial issues surrounding me when I hit number 715. I felt great about hitting that homer because a long ordeal for me had finally ended. I hoped, as I was rounding the bases and the fans were cheering, that I'd be able to put behind me all of the hostility that had built up to that point. It was as if because I was black, I had no right to break Babe's record. Among the things that bothered me the most was over 900 pieces of racist and vicious hate mail I received. The letters were downright ugly, and the feelings weren't anything that the senders were trying to hide. They would start out each letter by saying "Dear Nigger" this and "Dear Nigger" that, "I hope you never make it to the ballpark." They threatened me, my family at home, and my daughter who was in college. This is what I had to go through at the time. I hoped, when I saw that ball head into the stands, that maybe the people who were writing these letters would get on with their lives once I hit 715 and leave me alone. Believe it or not, that feeling of relief was the most predominant thing I was thinking about as I headed for home plate on that day.

When I replaced Bobby Thomson because he broke his ankle, many asked me my gut feelings at the time. Well, I can't really recall all the details. I did feel sorry for Bobby Thomson, but it put me in the position where I could perform in the majors. It so happens I played with a manager named Charlie Grimm, who was not a robot-type manager. He told me, "Kid, the job is yours, so get out there and do the best job you can." And that's what I did.

Who had the greatest influence on my baseball career? I think the one manager that I can remember was the first manager I ever played for, Ben Gerraghty of the Jacksonville team. I was one of the first blacks playing in the Sally League. I was literally going through hell down there. Name calling, racial slurs, resentment for playing against whites. So many stupid things. Ben used to come over to the hotel and talk to me and just give me the inspiration and the things I needed to carry on and be a professional baseball player.

There have been some changes for the black players since 1954, but of course we still have a long way to go. We now have bigger salaries for the bigger players, but outside of that I don't think there have been any significant changes in club management on the executive level.

As to how I feel as a black man in breaking Babe Ruth's record, really, I didn't look upon it as a black or white breaking a record. I thought about it as a ballplayer who had the ability to play ball for twenty years. The record was there, and I happened to be the one who was in a position to challenge it, and I wasn't going to pass it up, so I broke it. I hope some kid will come along and break mine.

And I am still waiting for total integration for the black ballplayer in the major leagues. For that to happen there will have to be some things done. We're just standing still, like stagnant water. I think we have proven to the baseball world and everybody else that we can perform on the field and if given the chance we can perform just as well in the front office. So these are some of the changes that have to be made. And I think the only way some of them can be made is not only through baseball but through some civil rights organizations like NAACP and PUSH which are going to have to step in and do a lot of things. Of course, the problem is that some of these organizations do not understand our position as to whether or not we are satisfied with what's happening.

Now that I'm in management, I still don't see the big changes that by rights should have taken place in baseball since 1947 when Jackie Robinson broke into the majors. I don't meet other black senior executives in baseball front offices because they don't exist. I'm senior vice president of the Braves organization, but I can't shake hands with other black managers in the rank and file positions because I'm alone. I don't see many black coaches, which is a shame considering the number of black players in the league today. And through all the years, we've had only four black managers. That's far too few. Whatever changes have taken place since 1947 are only window dressing.

From where I sit, and I've been involved in management since 1976, I don't see that much improvement for black people at all. At present we have Hal McRae managing in Kansas City and Cito Gaston up in Toronto, but there are no other persons beside myself in the team front offices. Of course, Bill White is the National League president, but that's like a little grain of salt. I want to see a much greater representation. What we need to see are blacks getting involved in the actual day-to-day running of the game: many more black managers, more black people in the front offices, and a far greater number of black coaches. We need to see opportunities open up for African Americans throughout the entire organization of professional baseball.

Today's baseball teams own many separate franchises and each franchise has hundreds of job openings for qualified people. For example, the Braves organization has a Triple-A team in Richmond, a Double-A team in Greenvale, and four or five Class-A franchises in other towns. Each of these separate teams has a variety of jobs which can be filled by black people who are not only ballplayers and managers.

You can employ black team physicians and trainers, blacks that launder the uniforms, people who work in the stadium, and people who work the concessions. There are so many places in the franchise system where qualified blacks do not have the opportunity to participate in this sport that it's an outrage. We can't call baseball an "All-American" sport and deny people the chance to work just because they're black.

Today, black superstars seem to have forgotten where they came from. They have the tendency to think that the door was always wide open for them from the beginning. But, if it hadn't been for a Don Newcombe, a Jackie Robinson, a Larry Doby, or any of the players who came before me, you would not have seen the likes of a Reggie Jackson, a Dave Winfield, or a Darryl Strawberry. These are the economic and historic realities of the past forty-five years.

I think that some of the younger black players in the league need history lessons. They have to understand that why they're here is not only because of their ability to play the game. They made it to the big leagues because people laid down their lives for them to make their millions of dollars. Accordingly, younger players should get involved again with the NAACP and with some of the black civil rights groups. They don't have to give money per se, but they have to get back in touch with what these groups stand for and look seriously at what it took for these groups to achieve all that they did.

When you start talking about why I'm here, why I can stay at this hotel, how far I've been able to come, the mere fact that I'm able to drink a glass of water in a public place, you're talking about Dr. King, Jackie Robinson, Malcolm X, and Andy Young. You're talking about civil rights people who worked hard so we can have an opportunity to be where we are. The young black athlete has got to learn about how he's gotten to where he's gotten today, and it isn't only because he's talented or gifted.

I dedicated my own book to Jackie Robinson because there was no way we would have had the opportunities if it weren't for him. He paved the way for all of us, and not just in baseball either. That's why when Vince Coleman says, "I don't know nothing about no Jackie Robinson," it makes me think he's a fool, a total fool. Yet if you asked him the same question about Babe Ruth, he'd say of course he knows who the Babe is. It's as if Coleman has forgotten the past and it saddens me to hear anybody who plays baseball say that he never heard of Jackie Robinson. All people should know what Jackie meant to people, both blacks and whites. There are too many players who would never have put on a major league baseball uniform had Jackie not walked through the door first and taken upon himself more abuse than any of us would ever take.

Jackie Robinson was special. He was the ideal pioneer because nobody else could have taken the level of the abuse that was thrown at him. He was a highly intelligent person not only as a player but also as a human being, and graced with the understanding that enabled him to have withstood the personal attacks he endured. He knew he was cutting a trail and had to be the focus of bigotry and frustration. I myself couldn't have handled what he faced, nor could most of the players who came after him such as Larry Doby, Don Newcombe, or even Roy Campanella. They were all pioneers in their own ways, but they followed the path of a unique trailblazer.

I have to give Branch Rickey all the credit for making sure that Jackie had the opportunity to play without folding under the pressure. I've heard from other players and people who were there that Rickey sat Jackie down and said, "No matter what happens—they can spit on you, they can kick you and call you names. You got to take it." I've experienced some of that same animosity off the field that Jackie did. I got angry! I was damned if I was going to let some white person come up to me and kick me or spit on me. I decided I never was going to let them treat me the way they treated Jackie in those early years.

It's bad enough to be taunted during a game when the spectators are legitimately paying the price of admission to hoot and holler at what's happening on the diamond. But after the game is over you expect there'll be some relief, that the fans will leave you alone. Jackie didn't have that luxury. For him the pressure had to have built up inside until the years of racism and hatred eventually took his life. It must have accumulated in him like a poison. Jackie died at a very early age. He was in his fifties and never had the chance to live his life the way he deserved. It's clear that the kind of racism he endured took its toll on him after he left the game. It was a shame.

A few years after Jackie Robinson established himself in the majors, there came along a really powerful player named Monte Irvin. He was a big, gifted ballplayer. Monte had the ability to do everything on the field: run the bases, steal, hit with power, catch, and throw out runners from either left or right. Monte belonged to a group of gifted players that included men like Cool Papa Bell and Josh Gibson—men whom America treated by the color of their skin rather than by the strength of their talents. Because of racism Americans allowed a previous generation of black ballplayers to go right down the drain without ever having the opportunity to play big-league ball. It was clearly a missed opportunity for the American fans as well as for the players. It was Jackie Robinson's courage that helped change all that.

I once said in an interview years ago that after my ballplaying days were over, I wouldn't want to be a "house boy," to put it bluntly. Back then I would have been able to forget about baseball and work for Magnavox, with whom I'd developed a good relationship during my playing days. There were other business ventures where I could have done as well, but I decided to stay in baseball. I was disappointed, though, because of the lack of front office positions available to black athletes. I believed, and still do, that once a black ballplayer takes off his uniform, he has nothing to do. Doors close in his face. Maybe he's made a lot of money, but after his career's over he can't do anything constructive in management to affect club policy. I'm trying to change this.

I'm a senior vice president with the Braves. I work directly for Ted Turner, who has told people that he's my boss and that I report to no one else. He told me the only thing he wants me to do is write my reports on each player and on the club, sit on the CNN board, and sit on the Braves board. I have one office at the Braves and another at CNN; I have two secretaries, and I'm my own man inside both organizations. I'm an example. If I can work in a front office position after my playing days, so can hundreds of other talented black ballplayers who can put the experience they've gained on the field into directing the future of the game.

Part of the problem is perception. Most black players are translated to the public and then back to themselves through the white media. Therefore, if there is a common perception that blacks can't make it to the front office—even when it's a false perception that's based on old racism—people believe it. I'm trying to break that perception and change the way people think. Specifically, white ballplayers and the white media simply don't want to understand the subtle and obvious racism that all black people have to face. For example, Eddie Matthews, who was one of my old teammates on the Braves, once said about me that if he had known about my "problems" when we were on the same team, he would have stepped forward to be friends. But the problem wasn't with me. It was with Eddie Matthews. He's the one who didn't step forward. I was right there all the time.

Eddie and some of the other players on the Braves back then said they didn't know me. But I say that unless you walk a mile in a man's shoes, you can't know that man. We were all on the same team, but they didn't take the opportunity to learn what I was about. Nobody on the Braves knew what I was going through at the time because the opportunities they took for granted, I had to fight for every single day.

Black players sometimes get a reputation for being hostile. They're not hostile. They just see the world through their own eyes. When people ask why a particular black person might be militant or angry, I answer that one shouldn't judge an individual until he knows what the man's thinking and what he's experienced. You can't judge anybody until you know who you're dealing with. For me, growing up in Alabama meant dealing with a racist and hostile enemy. That helped shape the way I thought and acted when I was younger.

I can recall things that happened to me as a little boy that have remained with me through the years. I can remember as clearly as anything one day when I was a fifteen-year-old kid in Mobile, Alabama, sitting in the house with my mother who was lying in bed with my little sister. The cops burst right in through the door. They didn't need a warrant or anything. They just stomped into the room and dumped my mother and sister right on the floor. I knew what was going on all right, but I said even then something's got to be wrong. You just don't treat people like this. I walked out to the back to get a pump handle and the only person who stopped me was my brother. Both he and I knew very well that if I'd gone back in there with that pump handle, I would have been one dead soldier.

Those kinds of images and memories stay with you forever. Therefore, white people never really understand what happened to black people in this country because they simply weren't there. And black people have not been liberated to the point where we can experience our total freedom. There is simply a big gap of understanding and awareness between the races that won't go away until white people make an effort to understand what black people have experienced.

Hank Aaron was elected to the Baseball Hall of Fame in 1982.

FRANK ROBINSON

"The only reason I'm the first black manager is because I was born black."
Frank Robinson

ROBINSON INDIANS' MANAGER
New York Post headline, October 3, 1974

1st BLACK MANAGER: IT'S FRANK ROBINSON
New York Daily News, headline, October 4, 1974

INDIANS NAME ROBINSON FIRST BLACK MANAGER
The New York Times, headline, October 4, 1974

"What changed around here the most and made us the team we are today was the arrival of Frank in 1966. He put our club over the hump. We came close, but we never won until he came to Baltimore. He solidified the club. We were a good team before. We became a better team when he joined us. We became a great team when he came to know us and how much he could do for all of us. Leadership isn't a matter of color, it's a matter of how much of yourself you're willing to give to another man and how much of you he is willing to accept. Frank gave everything of himself and we accepted everything he gave us."

Brooks Robinson

On October 3, 1974, twenty-seven years after Jackie Robinson broke baseball's color ban by becoming one of the four hundred players then in the major leagues, it finally happened. At a crowded news conference in Cleveland Stadium, with the poise that has characterized his career as a slugger of almost six hundred home runs and as a clubhouse leader, Frank Robinson was named by the Cleveland Indians as major league baseball's first black manager. He received a one-year contract. The thirty-nine-year-old Robinson was chosen to succeed Ken Aspromonte as the American League team's twenty-eighth manager and Cleveland's ninth player-manager—the most of any major league team.

Then-president Gerald Ford described Robinson's selection as "welcome news for baseball fans across the nation" and a "tribute to Robinson personally, to his athletic skills and his unsurpassed leadership." Baseball Commissioner Bowie Kuhn said, "We got something done that we should have done before." Phil Seghi, the Indians' general manager, in announcing his selection declared, "Frank Robinson has the qualities that I was searching for in a manager, not because he was black or white. He has all the leadership qualities necessary to lead a major league ball club. You know what he did in Baltimore! He's a true leader."

Robinson helped the Baltimore Orioles represent the American League in four World Series in his six seasons there. He led the Cincinnati Reds to one National League pennant. He is the only major leaguer selected the Most Valuable Player in both leagues. Through twenty-one seasons with Cincinnati, Baltimore, Los Angeles, California, and Cleveland, he had a career batting average with .294; 2,943 hits, and 1,812 runs batted in. Robinson became the major leagues' first playing manager since Solly Hemus of the St. Louis Cardinals in 1959. Eddie Joost, with the Philadelphia Athletics in 1954, was the American League's last playing manager.

ROBBY'S DEBUT A HIT
Homers as DH; Indians Ax Yanks, 5-3
New York Daily News, headline, April 9, 1975

Robinson managed Santurce in the Puerto Rican Winter League for five seasons. In those five seasons his teams finished first twice, third twice, and fourth once. When he joined Santurce for the 1968–69 season, he was the first American black to manage an integrated team of white, black, and Latin players.

Robinson was born in Beaumont, Texas on August 31, 1935, the youngest of ten children. A year later the family moved

to California. At fourteen he played American Legion ball.
When he was seventeen, after graduating from high school, the
Cincinnati Reds signed him for a $3,000 bonus. He played minor
league ball in Ogden, Utah; in the Pioneer League in 1953, Tulsa
of the Texas League in 1954, and with Columbia of the Sally
League in 1954 and 1955. It was in Columbia, which he describes as the "dark side" of his baseball career, where he said he
was first called "dirty nigger" after striking out. It was in
Columbia where he picked up a baseball bat and went into the
grandstands after some fans who were cursing him.

He joined the Reds in 1956 and became the National
League's Rookie of the Year. His thirty-eight home runs tied him
with Wally Berger of the 1930 Braves (Most Home Runs Hit by
a Player in His Rookie Season). He stood very close to the plate,
his bat held high and tight and unwavering. As a result, that same
season he established the major league record for being hit by
pitched balls: twenty.

He was named Most Valuable Player in the National
League in 1961. On December 9, 1965, Cincinnati traded him to
the Baltimore Orioles for outfielder Dick Simpson and pitchers
Milt Pappas and Jack Baldschun. He was traded, contended the
Reds' General Manager Bill De Witt, "because he was an old
thirty." Yet in his first year with the Orioles, in 1966, he led the
American League in batting, home runs, and runs batted in. In
1967 he became the eighth player to reach the $100,000-a-year
salary mark, following Joe DiMaggio, Ted Williams, Stan Musial, Willie Mays, Mickey Mantle, Sandy Kaufax, and Don
Drysdale.

Robinson's brilliant Oriole career terminated in 1972,
when he was traded to the Los Angeles Dodgers. In 1973 the
Dodgers sent him to the California Angels, who shipped him in
the late 1974 season to the Cleveland Indians. Robinson is fourth
on the all-time home run list with 586, surpassed only by Hank
Aaron, Babe Ruth, and Willie Mays.

FRANK ROBINSON: What Jackie did was so much more important than what I'm doing. . . . In 1947 it was a breaking period for black people coming back into baseball, and how many followed depended so much on Jackie's conduct. But that's not the case now. What and how I do doesn't mean nearly as much as what and how Jackie did . . .

Frank Robinson was elected to the Baseball Hall of Fame in 1982.

FERGUSON JENKINS

Ferguson Jenkins is a tall, lean, right-handed flame-thrower who played seventeen seasons in the major leagues, most of them with the Chicago Cubs. Fergie had a patented low-and-away breaking ball that drove National League batters to fits when they tried to golf after it or dig it out of the very edge of the strike zone. Jenkins' career 264 wins is even more impressive when you realize that he played most of his home games at Chicago's Wrigley Field where there were no lights. Thus, all of Fergie's home Chicago wins were during the day when the ball was easier to hit because it didn't have a nighttime haze that sometimes confuses batters and makes the pitcher's job easier.

"He's an artist. He just paints the corner of the plate pitch after pitch."
Jim Sundberg

"Location and changing speeds are the names of my game. If you can't pitch high and low, in and out in this game, you can't survive."
Ferguson Jenkins

Some of Fergie's most dramatic moments on the field took place during the 1969 season when the Cubs under Leo Durocher tried valiantly to fight off the New York Mets' end-of-the-year charge through the National League playoffs and into the World Series. The Mets won the fall classic that year by beating the Orioles in five games. Durocher tried everything to put the Cubs over the top in '69, but it was the year of the Amazin's. Jenkins pitched right into the teeth of the Mets' ferocious batting order, putting his strikes across corners of the plate where you'd have to have a sixth sense to find them. But that Mets team was a powerhouse and went on into the record books.

Jenkins went into history too, especially when he made the difficult transition from the National League to the Texas Rangers of the American League and faced not batters, but umpires with thicker chest pads that prevented them from looking down to see where Fergie's most effective pitch crossed the plate. As a result, Jenkins experienced the real horror of "knowing" he was throwing strikes but watching as the umps kept saying, "Sorry, Fergie, too low." But Jenkins was the type of competitor who always kept on trying to put the ball over and eventually they began calling his strikes again. He, too, went on into history.

FERGUSON JENKINS: That '69 season I played on a team with Ernie Banks, Billy Williams, Ron Santo, Glen Beckert, Randy Hundley, Kenny Holtzman, Bill Hands, and manager Leo Durocher. We were a great team but we were outmatched by the 1969 New York Mets, who stormed their way into history. They played sensational ball, winning some twenty-eight or thirty games during August and September, and chalking up a remarkable record. They were playing .800 ball, and we just didn't recover from it.

We lost one series to Philadelphia, another to the Cardinals, and still another to the Mets who simply overtook us like an express train. Once we got into second place, we couldn't fight our way back. Leo Durocher was becoming increasingly frustrated and kept saying that he wanted to back a truck up to the locker room and get rid of us. He said, "Well, if you guys are that tired, you might as well throw the towel in." But we weren't that tired; we just got outplayed by a lot of good ball clubs that were trying to knock off the winner. They were all spoilers who were eventually outplayed by the Mets.

Our morale on the Cubs remained high during that stretch as we watched the Mets gaining on us. We could see the race played out in each day's box scores in the newspapers in every city we visited. I remember we were going into Philadelphia and we were two-and-a-half games in front, but we lost the series, dropping three games in a row. The Mets were still a half game behind us. We went into New York for a do-or-die series that would decide the entire season. Tom Seaver and Jerry Koosman both beat us, and we lost three straight. We just didn't have the firepower to win our division. The Mets' superior pitching won them the National League Pennant and the World Series.

After twelve years in the National League, I was traded to the American League, where I had to make some significant adjustments because of the home-plate umpires. The American League umpires were still wearing the overinflated chest protector and couldn't really look down to call pitches at the bottom of the strike zone. During the first month that I was with the Texas Rangers I wasn't getting the same low strikes I would get in the National League. The umps knew I was throwing for the spot down and away, but they weren't giving it to me. I said to myself that I'd survived twelve years in the National League by throwing low strikes and down-and-away pitches in the zone and I wasn't going to change now. After a while, the umpires got used to those pitches and started to call them as strikes. I didn't have any problems after that.

My biggest problems started after I pitched those twenty win seasons in a row. You see, nobody really expected me to pitch so many twenty-game winning seasons. After the third, they thought I was in my prime; then came the fourth, the fifth, and the sixth years. The following year when I was 14-and-16, the Cubs thought my arm was gone so they traded me to the Texas Rangers, who were the last in their division in the American League. The same year I was traded, after the problems I had with the umpires and the strike zone, I won twenty-five games. So I proved to a lot of people who said I was finished that they were wrong. There were a lot of reporters who said I had hurt my arm or that my back was gone or something to that effect. But I kind of discounted that when I ended up winning those twenty-five games.

My career was ironic because I didn't originally come up to the majors as a starting pitcher. I was brought up in Philadelphia in '64 as a reliever even though I sat on the bench for the entire season. I didn't get the opportunity to pitch until '65 when the Phillies sent me to the mound in relief. The coaches had seen that I could throw strikes consistently the way I had done in Double-A and Triple-A ball. I could throw sliders and curveballs. I could control my down-and-away pitches and shut-out rallies by changing the tempo of a game. The important thing was that my pitches were always tight, especially when there were runners in scoring position. Then I could throw the strikes to make batters swing and get them to hit ground balls or pop ups. I always put out the fire. The Phillies traded me to Chicago in '66 where I won a lot of games as a reliever. In '67 the Cubs put me in the starting rotation and it enhanced my abilities while I made them more money.

Ferguson Jenkins was elected to the Baseball Hall of Fame in 1991.

RICKEY HENDERSON

It's the 1987 season and New York Yankee Rickey Henderson is complaining about a sore hamstring. They don't believe him. Yankee Manager Lou Piniella accuses Henderson of "jaking it." Nigger ball players are not supposed to get hurt. They play no matter what.

RICKEY HENDERSON: One hundred thirty stolen bases in 1982 was a titillating thing for me to have accomplished. Much of the credit for what I achieved belongs to Billy Martin, who told me in spring training that we were going to set the record that year and that was that. Billy had spoken! It was an exhilarating moment when I broke the record, and I'm still thrilled by it.

I owe my success mostly to manager Billy Martin, who inspired, was like family to me, and who was the best man I ever knew in my life. Billy was a great manager and individual who changed the way baseball was played. Many of his critics only knew him for the reputation he had or for the escapades he pulled. But I loved Billy Martin, and it broke my heart when he got killed in his truck.

In 1987 I had a hamstring problem and nobody understood that I was injured. Lou Piniella said that I was "jaking it." I truly feel that if I were Caucasian I would have been on the disabled list so fast you wouldn't have believed it. But even as recently as five years ago you couldn't be black and be hurt in this league. When I first pulled the muscle I didn't know what a hamstring problem was. If I could have called it something medical, they might have taken me seriously when I complained about the pain. But because I didn't have a name for it, people said I was slacking off.

I understand now that the Yankees needed me to play worse than they needed me to be healthy. I know how that sounds, but it's true. Team managers feel that black ballplayers can't get hurt, must always say they're healthy, and must report every day as if they don't have a care in the world. Blacks in this game must play by different standards than whites—no injuries, no pain, no complaints. Only the white players are allowed to sprain a muscle or pull a tendon. When we do get hurt, we only have a few days to get better. Those are the rules we have to play under and young black players learn those rules fast if they want to stay in baseball.

In the future I want to see more black ballplayers become managers and coaches because they will be better able to relate to the issues concerning minority players. It might be the only way for black and Hispanic players to get the fair shake they deserve. Unfortunately I don't see much hope for it because I think that owners don't believe that we have the knowledge or the ability to do the job. That saddens me because I know it's not true.

BILLY SAMPLE

Billy Sample played major league baseball for the Texas Rangers and the New York Yankees, where he established himself as a power hitter and an excellent fielder. After his playing days were over Sample became a sports commentator for ESPN. He is articulate and intelligent and not afraid to voice his opinions. He is an example of a newer generation of players who aren't content to accept the status quo. As a result, Sample was often branded a troublemaker or a clubhouse lawyer. But Billy Sample stood his ground and may eventually become one of the more outspoken commentators in baseball now that he's off the field and in the pressbox.

BILLY SAMPLE: Racism persists in baseball and predominates in all aspects of the game in both subtle and obvious ways. For example, here's a shocking story that's typical of the experiences black athletes have. When I was in spring training with the Texas Rangers I knew a black guy who was seeing a young white lady. A sports writer who knew both of them and knew they were seeing each other said directly to the young women, "How can you date a nigger?" Then I saw how his feelings about the woman's dating a black were becoming encompassed in his supposed "objective" analysis of this player to the degree where not only the player, but the woman and the writer knew what was happening. That was just the first taste that I had of the impact of racism when I was getting to the major leagues. And this is a relatively recent story.

My own story is equally revealing. My wife is white, and in Texas we had four years of death threats and harassment. This was a shame because even though there were some beautiful people in Texas, the historic vehicles to exhibit racism still existed. People who did it to the extreme would call the ballpark and threaten that they were going to kill my wife that night. They wanted to make it as difficult and painful for us as possible because my wife is white and they wanted to discourage our kind of relationship. But Joe Klein, a former general manager of Texas, after hearing that I was having those kinds of problems, asked me whether I wanted to be traded. I said, "No, Joe, I want more playing time. If I can't get more playing time, then get me out." I told him that I can't run away from this situation. And in an ironic sense this helped to strengthen my marriage.

I "graduated" from the playing field to the pressbox where I look around me and see only white faces. I look at the press corps that covers the sport and I see an overwhelming sea of white. It leads me to ask: Can black ballplayers get a fair shake from the white media? It certainly would be nice to have more black reporters writing about the game. They would be more representative of the opinions of black players who comprise a significant percentage of the team rosters. It would be nice to see more women, especially women from minority groups, reporting the game because they would tend to have more empathy with the minority players.

Minority players know the unspoken rule: In the minor leagues, if you're black or Hispanic you know that you have to be just a little bit better than the white man to advance. I don't know if that's because of out-and-out racism or if economics also plays a role. The demographics show that 94 percent of the fans that come to the ballpark are white and that the teams gear themselves to the overwhelming majority of the audience. Therefore, is it racism or is it purely economics that underlies decisions about player personnel? I believe it's both and that one feeds the other.

In baseball it's easier to make racist judgments and couch them in "objective" evaluations simply because player evaluations in baseball, statistics notwithstanding, are more subjective than they are in other sports. Baseball isn't like football where you can objectively see if a guy runs a strong 100 yards or not. If you want to see who's faster at running a pass pattern, you throw the pass and you clock the receivers downfield. Also baseball's not like basketball where a guy has a 47-inch vertical jump that's there for all to see. If you want to see who has a greater percentage from the free throw line, you can match players shot for shot. Much of baseball talent, however, is comparable. It is based on the relative assessments between players on a roster. Thus, if you want to hide racism, you can do it in a subjective analysis that is subsequently written out in objective language.

Because black players are sometimes the victims of injustices, when they react and seek change they're labeled "clubhouse lawyers." Among management, "clubhouse lawyer" is a fashionable term. It's an easy way to dismiss the complaints of a player who might be challenging the "good old boy" network that has come down from generation to generation. There has been a slow change for the better over the years. But sometimes you have to force change, and that's when these guys speak up.

"Clubhouse lawyer" is also a term that's meant to keep people in line. I've worn the title of clubhouse lawyer a couple of times and I think it stems from the fact that when a black ballplayer speaks up, people call him a troublemaker. If a black ballplayer tries to represent his own ideas and openly discusses what he sees as the things that need to be changed, they call him a clubhouse lawyer. He's accused of being pushy and creating dissension. I can understand this.

Since 1947 we've only had about four managers, very few coaches, one senior executive, and only one league senior executive. That's why I found the Campanis statements of a few years ago so offensive to all minority players. Al said that blacks don't have the necessary qualifications to be managers and coaches. It was a demeaning thing to say because black people have been excluded from that inner circle of decision making, so no one can judge whether blacks had the necessities that Campanis was talking about or not. But for Campanis to say what he did only perpetuates a situation in which blacks are denied the opportunity to participate.

Willie Stargell described the problem accurately when he asked, "How do you think we guys learned the game?" How do you think Art Howe learned the game? Don't you think blacks know how to play the game? Certainly all of what black players contribute to their teams and to the sport is not simply talent or prowess; it's knowledge and experience. So what Campanis is saying is a pure fallacy. We know it's a fallacy, but it's a matter of getting close enough to management in order to land positions of power. So far you have Bill White as the National League President, and it's a good move. But you wonder whether it's an appeasement or a token job because besides White you only have

Bob Watson, the Bull, who's the assistant GM in Houston, and Henry Aaron on the Braves. Where are the other black executives? They don't exist. That's a shame because I know a lot of talented black people, both physically and mentally, who are in positions where they should ascend to the next level.

It's hard enough to reach the ranks of management in the first place. Racism only increases the burden. Therefore I'm hoping that baseball will take care of itself so you won't have a big issue over which people on opposing sides will say: "Here we are and let's fight over this." Advancement for blacks in the sport shouldn't be an issue that has to be contested every few years because whites refuse to move unless they're pushed. But you do have to have something to maintain pressure on those people keeping blacks out of managerial positions because baseball is by nature very traditional.

DAVE WINFIELD

Dave Winfield looks like an ageless legend. He's a tall, powerfully built man who has all the gifts of a superb all-around athlete. Winfield is a consummate baseball player because he really can do it all. He hits for power and for position—one of the very few hitters in the big leagues who can make adjustments depending on the game situation. He moves runners around the bases as if they're on a conveyor belt and brings them home with determination and precision hitting. Winfield is a strong base runner despite the lower back problems that have plagued him, and he can catch anything that's hit near him. Winfield is also blessed with a howitzer arm that can pick runners off who are imprudent enough to run on him. Winfield is known for his commitment to the team and the game. He is one of the rare athletes who can go out on the field, day after day, and give 110 percent. In so doing, he's an inspiration to the other players on the team and sometimes, by sheer determination alone, Dave can make impossible things happen on the field.

As a Yankee, Dave had his share of controversies with George Steinbrenner. He wasn't the first player to have had them. Yet Dave rose above the conflicts and the kind of press those conflicts generated to a grander stature. Watching him run the bases with aggressiveness and skill was in itself more than worth the trip uptown to Yankee Stadium. Seeing him go out on the field to inspire the Yankees when you knew that his back was hurting him or that there was a new controversy in the Yankee dugout or front office was to see a legend being created before your eyes.

Dave is not just a hitter—there are plenty of hitters—he is a smart hitter. Winfield can intimidate pitchers with his power at the plate, especially as a DH, so that they worry about him instead of who else is on base. When pitchers make that mistake, they discover it too late. Dave understands the threat of being in scoring position and knows how the constant pressure of runners on second or third can soften up an infield and cause outfielders to make critical mistakes in judgment. That's why Winfield is the consummate player—he can beat you with his brains as well as with his bat, his throwing arm, his glove, or his legs.

There is another side of Dave Winfield that is sometimes overlooked during the frenzy of a season: Winfield the sensitive individual who wore the Yankee pinstripes with pride and dignity. There were a lot of ugly things said about Winfield, a lot of insinuations raised in the press by people he was negotiating with, and a lot of hardball playing off the field as well as on. Yet Winfield remained above the controversy, continued to go out on the field, continued to play despite the pain from his hurting back, and defied the commentators and sportswriters who said that he was simply too old to be a money player. Dave will always be a clutch player who demonstrates what baseball is supposed to look like when it's played at the highest levels of skill. Now playing for the Angels, Winfield just completed one of the greatest seasons in his career. He has also joined the record books as one of the few players who have successfully completed the "cycle:" a single, double, triple, and home run in one complete game. Whenever the Angels play in the "House that Ruth Built," the New York fans cheer him as one of their own, and his bat reminds the Yankees of the nemesis that they traded away every time he steps into the batters' box against their pitchers.

DAVE WINFIELD: George Steinbrenner once said that he made a big mistake in letting Reggie Jackson go and keeping me because he claimed I wasn't a clutch ballplayer. I've thought about that and realized that if he believed he'd made a mistake in letting Reggie go, then it's his mistake. It had nothing to do with me. I don't have to sit around the locker room and justify my being a clutch player. We are different kinds of players. With Reggie, you love him or you hate him because he would either come through and shine tremendously or be a bust. But he was "electric." The fans always were confident that he could produce at exactly the right time as he did in all those post-season games with the A's and then with the Yankees. Nobody has to be reminded of October, 1976.

But after Reggie, the Yanks weren't in too many post-season games, so I really can't make that kind of a comparison between us. George may have wanted Reggie on the roster because he's going to attract fans and hit the big home run that fans like so much. But as far as consistency and bigger numbers, I put them on the board every year. I'm an all-around ballplayer.

From the perspective of the years that I've put into the sport, I can assess—both as a player and a black athlete—what's going on in big league-ball today. There are two aspects to a sport: what happens on the field, which is what the fans see, and what happens off the field, which no one sees. I may make the game look easy when I'm in the stadium, which is what you're supposed to do if you're an athlete, but that has very little bearing on what goes on behind the scenes. People don't know and may not care what goes on in the locker room among the players and coaches, in the board rooms where decisions are made, or in negotiations where there's a whole world of baseball that no one is allowed to enter except players, agents, lawyers, and management.

That's the business behind the sport, and it's rougher than the sport itself. Baseball is far less a game than it is big business, and players who come up to the majors and don't understand that are in for the shock of their lives. There are people I've encountered in the business of baseball who play more aggressive hardball than pitchers I've faced at home plate.

Where I've succeeded I've done so because of my friends in the major leagues who gave me good advice. Willie McCovey was one such player who really helped me out with the honesty of his opinions. I respected his stature both as an athlete and as a human being, and he taught me a lot. I've also learned from the Joe Morgans, the Lou Brocks, and the Hank Aarons; those quality ballplayers whose reputations, demeanors, and characters served as fine examples.

I've tried to glean information and knowledge from all the teams I've played on, the minor league cities I've worked in, and the athletes I've competed with. I gained a lot of insights into the "psychology" of a baseball team, what makes it tick, and how players relate to each other. I traveled quite a bit and had different experiences with each new encounter. Therefore, I wasn't overwhelmed when I came to the major leagues. I have a good family and friends who've become a supporting mechanism for me.

And my mentor—the guy who also turned out to be my agent—David Al Frohman, also helped me quite a bit by suggesting that I try new things and even put myself out on a limb. If I were hesitant about something, he'd say, "Just go there. Do this. Try that." He made me aware when new opportunities were crossing my path.

You'd be surprised how much you can discover if you keep your ears open and get involved with what's going on around you. When Al and I would negotiate a contract, it wasn't as if he were someone going off and representing me all by himself and saying, "Wait two more hours and when I come back it'll be over." I was a part of the process and contributed to the strategy.

I further broadened my knowledge of the sport by getting involved in union activities. I understood from being a player representative that baseball is a game, a business, and a science at the same time. All of this taught me to think about major league ball, to be intellectual about it as well as instinctive. I trained myself to become better by making myself more aware of what was going on around me both during a game and during negotiations between players and management. I figured out that you can develop timing and balance and other skills that enhance your ability to play and give you longevity.

So when people say that I am just a streak hitter or that I'm a free swinger, it's just the opposite. I consider myself a thinker who adapts to new conditions. I trained myself to be the kind of guy that I would want to play with on my team by developing a variety of skills that typify an all-around substantial player who contributes. That's the player I want to play with and the player I try to be.

I've had my anxious moments, especially in New York, where it was much more difficult than it ever should have been. But I was never the individual who creates the problems on a team. Neither was I a clubhouse lawyer, nor the fool who doesn't play hard or who fluctuates tremendously from season to season and acts as if he doesn't care because they gave him the money and he doesn't have to do anything to earn it.

I don't come into the locker room drunk or high as other players sometimes do. I'm always ready to play. I stay consistent. That's what I mean by being the kind of guy I'd like to have on my team.

I have a lot of pride and when times are tough it's what keeps me going. I don't argue or fight all the time. Rather, I protect myself and what I believe in. That was one of the reasons I had so much trouble during the rough years on the Yankees. I thought that for maybe one or two years in my career in New York I'd be able to play without the duress and the distractions which are unnecessary and which take you off your game. But it didn't work out that way no matter how hard I tried to avoid a confrontation. New York really is a pressure cooker, and when you are a professional athlete in this town, you're under a microscope and an X-ray camera at the same time.

I've experienced racism in my life. It was all around me when I was on the Yankees and competing with Don Mattingly for the batting title. Here we both were, two guys on the same team, fighting one another for the same thing against a background of manipulative media and the perceptions of hundreds of thousands of fans that were created by that media. There was a vast difference in the amount of encouragement each of us got from the press and the public. And the stories that flew between us were blown out of all proportion. It was disheartening to listen to and be subjected to the discussion at the time, but it was an experience that taught me a lot. It was rough, it was nasty, and I could really see where people were coming from.

One way to combat racism in baseball is to have more blacks in all sectors and jobs in the sport. We have to have the opportunities we think are there whether they be in management, on the field, in the front offices, or even in the media that reports the game. What's the percentage of blacks in jobs in front offices? Four percent? Eight percent? Probably less. It's too small and it has to change. I believe that the situation will improve in time just like I believe that we'll have more than four black managers in the major leagues. But we have to make it improve. We can't sit back and wait for it to happen, and it's not going to happen all by itself.

Some of the managers are hiring more blacks and other minority coaches for their staffs, so there is some activity. And you have to hand it to the managers who are looking for black and minority coaches because they are trying to make the situation better. Sooner or later these coaches, once they have experience on the field, will have the opportunity to be managers. I hope we'll be able to see a whole new generation of black managers that may well include Reggie, who's now a coach, and myself.

Baseball is America's sport and it has to reflect what's happening in America. In ten years there should be a lot of opportunity for black people in all aspects of baseball franchises and league operations. By rights, we should be seeing great progress for blacks in baseball precisely because it is America's sport. If progress continues at the same slow pace, then something's terribly wrong. I'm going to teach my kids to have something to do with this game because I want them make a contribution to what I love to do best in the world. For myself, maybe I can be like Jack Benny and never turn forty.

DAVE PARKER

Dave Parker plays for the California Angels. He was traded from Pittsburgh where, during the 1978 season, fans at the Pirates stadium hurled flashlight batteries down at him as he tried to play the outfield. The fans were ejected from the stands and there were the usual nostros culpae in the press, but the incident stands as one of the ugliest racial incidents in modern baseball. The incidents started when Dave Parker became one of the highest paid baseball players by breaking the million-dollar salary barrier. Fans were furious that a black player was the first to earn this much money as a player. Dave Parker's experiences as the victim of this form of racism always reminds me of some of the experiences Jackie Robinson, Roy Campanella, Don Newcombe, Larry Doby, Cleon Jones, and Henry Aaron faced on the field. What happened to Dave Parker in 1978 shows that we haven't come that far since 1947.

Dave Parker: The battery incidents in the stadium took place during a time of great frustration for the city of Pittsburgh when all local business was in decline, especially the steel industry. People couldn't accept the economic issues of the supply and demand of labor. The fact that I had received $1 million to play the game of baseball created a lot of resentment and I was the object of much hostility. But it was also an indication of the resentment that was generally pervasive throughout the city because of what was happening. Everybody was getting hurt as the recession and inflation whipsawed the local economy. People were losing their jobs and the unions couldn't protect them. I also realize that the simple fact that I was black made the situation quite a bit worse.

There were players—white players—who were not as good as Dave Parker at the time but who were still close to that $1 million bracket. But because the Pirates considered me to be the best player in the game, my being a black guy during very frustrating economic times brought out a lot of resentment from the public. Much of that lay behind the battery-throwing incident. I could have gotten seriously injured, and it still scares me to think about it.

I haven't given a lot of thought to staying in baseball after I retire as a player maybe because I'm enjoying the Angels so much. I spend a lot of time away from my family and I think retirement would be time for me to catch up on that. But if the ideal job came along, I wouldn't mind managing in the majors or representing ballplayers. I think that during my tenure in Pittsburgh, the Players' Association wasn't completely supportive when I had lawsuits filed against me. I think it's time for the players to have an association where the personnel are more sympathetic to the black players' problems as they relate to baseball.

Where I think the biggest gains might lie, though, is in club ownership, which is a financial issue that I'd like to address some day. My idea would be to get together with some of the multi-million dollar players around and actually apply for a league franchise in a city. I think that's when and where the change is going to come. We have to become part of the institution itself, part of ownership, part of the rules committees. We have to become an integral part of the structure of the game. Look what happened in Denver with regard to that franchise. I was feeling very good about it until it collapsed.

DARRYL STRAWBERRY

"Darrrrryl," the fans would scream out in Shea Stadium. "Darrrrryl," they would hoot, drawing the R's in his name out as far as they could as if it were some kind of magical chant, a mantra, a love song. Every time Darryl Strawberry stepped up to the plate in baseball's media pressure-cooker, the fans would react. Would this be a home run? Would Darryl lift his right foot off the ground as the pitch came flaming towards him and whip his bat around and under the ball to send it sailing out of the park? That's what the fans came for, the press said, to see Darryl Strawberry hit home runs. And hit them he did. Darryl led the Mets and was one of the National League leaders for every one of his eight years on the New York Mets.

Darryl's statistics were so impressive that by the time he was only twenty-five people were saying that he would almost surely be one of the all-time greats of the sport. That's a tall order for anyone to fill. But when he was seventeen years old and playing in high school they were saying that about him as well. You have to realize what it's like for someone to be constantly compared to his potential future and to history. This is how it's been for Strawberry.

But Darryl, who in 1990 became the second highest paid baseball player of all time after he turned free agent and was signed by the Los Angeles Dodgers to a precedent-setting five-year contract, has tried to overcome his own future with good humor, style, grace, courage, spiritual devotion, and intensity. How can you play for the future when your only job is to move people around the bases and drive home the runners? You have to take one inning at a time, which is what Darryl Strawberry has tried to do.

Darryl is a big guy, a lot bigger than you'd think if you just watch him on the small screen. He towers over other players on the field and when he brings his long arms around the plate, it looks as though there's nothing that he can't hit. But that's also been one of the problems that's dogged him through the years. Because Darryl looks as though he can work miracles on the field, when he doesn't work them—because he's a human being like all the other players—people criticize. It takes a certain sense of grace and understanding to weather criticism. Even when you get the hits, as Darryl did in 1985 with a scoreboard busting home-run shot in the middle of a critical Mets series, and the team doesn't win in the end, it's your fault. "Why couldn't Darryl have done more?" the press insinuated over and over again.

Darryl Strawberry's unique abilities have made him seem larger than life. People talk about Darryl's third eye, his ability to sense when a runner is going to tag up and make a break even before the runner knows it. You don't want to be the runner breaking from second when Darryl gets his glove on the ball because by the time the idea pops into your brain to head for third, the ball's already there. And this is what has delighted fans at Shea and around the country.

Then there's Darryl's fielding. Like other superstars in the outfield, Darryl seems to know where a ball is going to wind up even as it leaves the bat. He doesn't just catch the ball, he seems to make the ball come to him; he wills it into his glove. Therefore, when a ball is legitimately hit over his head or takes the kind of bounce that's a fielder's nightmare, Darryl takes what can only be called a bad rap. That's the problem with being a legend before the history books are closed: Somehow you can never quite live up to what the press expects you to be because you're already a legend. Darryl has had to play under this burden in the toughest baseball city in the country, New York. That is, until he decided that it was time to go home to Los Angeles to play for the Dodgers.

Darryl Strawberry is still young enough for most fans to remember when he was in high school. Although Crenshaw High School is just another city school in the Los Angeles Unified School District, it seems that it has had more than its share of good baseball players. Darryl had previously played sandlot ball in his Crenshaw neighborhood when he was younger, and by the time he was only a sophomore in high school people around him were saying he was pro material. He was scouted while he was still in his first year on the team, scouted again the following year, and by the time he was a junior, he saw three senior members of the Crenshaw team get drafted into the pros. He says that's when he realized that he, too, could really make it to the pros. And that's exactly what happened. In 1980 a Mets team that was wallowing in the cellar of the National League picked Darryl as their number-one draft choice and the ride began.

Darryl has said consistently, and it's easy to believe him when you look at the press clippings, that his career was laid out for him by the press even before he got to New York. First there was the money, and lots of it. What does a seventeen-and-a-half-year-old high-school graduate do with all that money? How can you keep what in 1980 were huge bonuses from going right to your head? Darryl tried, but money seems to have a life of its own, and if you make too much of it too soon, the sportswriters will tell you that you've been overpaid. So Darryl was overpaid even before he cashed his first check.

Then there was the pressure of the expectations. Darryl has always said to anyone who took the time to listen that all he wanted to do was have "fun." Baseball itself was a game. Baseball was supposed to be a fun experience, the meeting of a ball with your bat on a lot in Crenshaw and feeling it sail out of the park. That was fun. But for a seventeen-year-old just out of high school, the pressure of being the savior of the New York Mets took much of the fun out of it. At first the press began to talk about the "Black Messiah" from Los Angeles, a tall order for anybody. Then the sports commentators said that Darryl was a "Black Ted Williams." These were heavy and eventually onerous expectations.

Darryl said at the time that he didn't want to fulfill any roles or preconditions. He said he understood what the Mets needed and what their hopes for him were. But he said that he also understood that he was ready to learn, ready to make the transformation from raw, natural talent to a major leaguer—a big jump in the 1980s. The game had grown more complicated, more sophisticated, and Darryl was going to spend his time in the minors learning what the big leagues were all about. That was the way he thought it would happen, but it didn't.

When Darryl was drafted number one, the Mets were still groping through the cellar. They were laughably inept. They needed power on the roster and Darryl was the only power in their future. New York sportswriters had been telling Frank Cashen to draft Strawberry even before Darryl's senior year was over, and Cashen had listened to their advice—as if he really needed that kind of advice to make his decision. But from the moment Darryl arrived in Kingsport, his first minor league team, the press began to howl. "Why is Darryl being wasted in the minors?" they asked as the Mets moved into a disastrous 1981 season. "Where's Darryl?" they clamored as Darryl was belting the hapless minor league pitchers out of the park while the Mets still languished in last place.

Finally, Darryl was moved up to Tidewater the following year as the Mets looked forward to another miserable season. Darryl said that he was able to hit minor league pitching easily because it was much like the pitching he had faced in high school, only faster. Minor league pitchers had more control than his high school pitchers. They tended not to get themselves into as much difficulty with their early pitches, Darryl said, and they made you work harder to get to the ball. But they were still throwing mostly fastballs and easy curves that broke away from you. These were the kinds of pitches he'd been hitting since his high school days and he had no trouble with them. Thus, Darryl's batting statistics were strong enough to make the New York press laugh with derision at Mets general manager Frank Cashen.

By the start of the 1983 season, the press had begun to bait Cashen. They beat him up with his own bonus player. "Why was he protecting Strawberry?" they asked. Was Darryl too good for the majors? Was Cashen afraid he'd made a mistake with this mysterious high school graduate who was touted as the next Ted Williams? The Mets could do nothing right, and when they told Darryl to fly to New York to meet the team and play against Cincinnati, there was an ominous feeling. This was going to be Strawberry's debut. After three seasons and change in the minors, the nineteen-year-old kid was going to take on major league pitching and assume the role of savior of the Mets.

It didn't quite work out that way. Darryl remembers watching as Cincinnati's Mario Soto whizzed three fast change-ups by him that seemed to have lives of their own. Darryl says that he had never seen pitching like this: balls that look like they're coming right over the plate and then suddenly drop like stones just as you're bringing your bat around. Darryl struck out three times that night and the press and fans booed him right off the field. So much for the bonus kid who would save the Mets. Darryl has said that inauspicious beginning with the Mets was a shock.

He soon learned to hit major league pitching so well that he paid Soto back for their first meeting. But the damage was done. Darryl had already gotten a bad reputation in the New York press for being something less than he was supposed to be and it dogged his career for the next seven years with the Mets. Even though Strawberry helped them into the 1986 World Series and into subsequent playoffs, he was never quite good enough for the press and the fans. When he hurt his back two years later and had to sleep on the floor because the pain was so intense and he couldn't move on the field with the same agility he had demonstrated in the past, critics said that he was goldbricking. When other players were hurt, baseball commentators sympathized; when Darryl got hurt, they said he was faking.

In the beginning of 1989, Darryl's agent, Eric Goldschmidt, had asked the Mets management a hypothetical question: What would happen to Darryl's next contract if he had a really big year in '89? The way free agency works, '89 was Darryl's guaranteed year and '90 was his option year. After 1990, Darryl could become a free agent and accept the highest offer from any club. Darryl said that he wanted to lock things up with the Mets if at all possible, so he'd asked Mets management—and that meant Frank Cashen—what they might do after the 1990 season. If they were of a mind to keep him on the team, maybe it would have been to everyone's advantage to write the contract extension now instead of waiting.

The New York press jumped all over Darryl, clamoring that Strawberry was trying to renegotiate his contract in spring training by holding a gun to the Mets' head. It was said in the close of 1988 that Darryl wanted to return to Los Angeles and he was looking for a way out. The Mets responded by saying that they would not renegotiate a contract extension and Darryl let the matter drop. But it was a burden that Darryl had to carry with him throughout the season every time he struck out or let a ball get by him. It was a burden Darryl had to carry as he moved into the 1990 season when the Mets front office suddenly decided to open up negotiations on his contract. Darryl learned all about it on the sports pages of the New York dailies because the Mets management, he says, had not informed him.

During the ensuing 1990 season, every time Darryl did something less than the impossible on the field, people said that he was letting down the team because he wanted to get more money on his next year's contract. Even his own teammates criticized him and there was talk of bitterness in the locker room and scenes of pushing and shoving on the ballfield. And it was all Darryl's fault, the press suggested. Fortunately or unfortunately, because Darryl has been so gifted as an athlete, he seems as though he can make the impossible happen. Therefore what he routinely accomplishes as a day-to-day ballplayer is just as routinely overlooked by writers who criticize him for not making magic happen.

Darryl has admitted that when he was on the Mets, that kind of criticism got to him. He was trying for the impossible, achieved some great numbers, but because he was always trying for the impossible he looked inconsistent. This is something he says he is trying to change now that he is with the Dodgers. He correctly perceives that the intense pressure is off him for a while. Darryl has said that playing at home in Los Angeles and playing for a manager like Tommy Lasorda will do wonders for his outlook.

In addition to the spiritual insight which he experienced at a prayer meeting in Anaheim, Darryl has also been through a dependency recovery program. His stint at Smithers before the 1990 season began, he said, helped open up his eyes to what he had done with his life and how he had let the pressure get to him. And his return to Los Angeles where he could get an early start on the season, he says, has helped him to acclimate himself to playing at home again and working out the muscles that need to be worked out before spring training begins.

Darryl looks remarkably comfortable at Dodger Stadium wearing number 44 and gracefully swatting long flies out to deep center field from the batter's box. You don't see the tension on his face that became etched in as soon as spring training began with the Mets. And Darryl's very auspicious start in Vero Beach's Dodgertown just weeks before the season began also presaged a more relaxed, more comfortable, even a more mature Darryl Strawberry. Maybe, he says, some of his old edge is gone, but he's more than happy with the reflectiveness and focus that he has found. Darryl has also said that he's working on being more consistent instead of a streak hitter, and that he has gotten support for what he's trying to do from people like Reggie Jackson, who has been there before and who understands what it's like when you're one of the highest paid players in the game and the fans get down on you.

Darryl has said that during his slump earlier in the 1991 season, Reggie Jackson telephoned him in the locker room and advised him to listen only to himself and not to the critics. Reggie told him that it was easy for people to criticize someone for making a lot of money and not producing to their expectations. Darryl isn't the first player to have to endure this. Reggie endured it before Darryl, and Hank Aaron, Cleon Jones, and Larry Doby endured it before Reggie. It's tough when you are so good you make it look easy, because it's not easy. And other black superstars who have had to face the criticism from a white press have learned that you can't live up to other people's expectations and you can't play someone else's game. You have to play your own game and be your own person.

After the 1991 All-Star Game, Darry blossomed and showed the kind of all-around contribution he could make. He helped the team with his sizzling bat and with his now mature leadership abilities. His efforts almost brought the Dodgers to the championship of the National League West.

As Darryl approaches the prime of his career, his decision to be his own person and play the game he knows will work for him will pay off in the end. Even though his decision to leave the Mets continues to rankle New York sports fans and baseball commentators, Darryl believes it was the best thing he could have done.

Darryl Strawberry: There was a part of me that was very sad to leave New York. The Mets had been my first major league team and I had many happy memories there, including a World Series Championship. As soon as I'd made my decision to take the Dodgers offer, the first person I spoke to was Dwight Gooden, who had been my friend through all my years in New York. Doc felt bad that I was leaving. He looked up at me when I put my hand on his shoulder and said, "You're leaving, you're gone." From the tone of his voice, I knew that he was sad. I told him "Doc, I had no choice." And he knew it.

Gooden always used to sit down and talk to me about the problems I was having on the Mets. He knew that the Mets never seemed to want to commit to me for the long term even though I'd been there for ten years. "How did they treat you?" he would ask. I told him that they would always take me down that same road by offering me a little while promising me a lot. "We'll give you a two-year contract," they would say to me. "And maybe a two-year extension." But I could look around and see them giving other players three- and four-year extensions and I would ask why. Finally it had gotten to the point where I was bitter just going into the locker room. It was time for the Mets to commit to me or to let me negotiate with the club that wanted me the most.

This was an "ethnic" problem, the same problem that other black ballplayers had faced. Frank Cashen never took the time to know me as a human being. He only saw me as a worker in his organization. We were supposed to belong to the same team, but it was a team that Frank wasn't on. He could have talked to me many times. But he never wanted to know anything about my feelings, even though he knew that I was always available to talk. All he wanted from me was just to "hit the baseball." Just produce.

The ironic thing about my years on the Mets was that I did produce. I did hit the baseball and kept on hitting. I was consistent over the years, which is exactly what they wanted. But, I found out that hitting the baseball wasn't the issue; being a human being was more important. This was the most important lesson I learned from my years on the Mets.

Doc Gooden and I used to look around and realize that we were the only two black "performers" on the team. We were there to produce wins for the Mets by our performances on the field. We looked around and realized there were only two of us and we'd understand with a chill that was just the way it was going to remain. There wouldn't be any more black ballplayers on the Mets. And this is in New York City, where more than half the people who live there belong to minorities. I realized that because the Mets treat their number-one player in a derogatory way, they would never go out to pick up additional black players. They'd already showed their hand.

You know it's a real possibility that if the racial situation had been different and if I could have gotten a five-year contract, which is what I really wanted the most, I would still be in New York. People say that I just wanted out, but that wasn't the case. Remember, Frank Cashen said that I wasn't worth the money. I was looking for that fifth year, that investment in me as a person, because after all, the Mets kept on saying that I had to win in order for the team to win. OK, translate that into a five-year contract. But they wouldn't. And they wouldn't even talk to me about it. I am not going to make any blanket statements about Frank Cashen as a person, but I can say that I do know one thing—Frank Cashen wasn't fair to me.

It's astounding to realize that there is still a double standard in professional baseball even today. So many years after Jackie Robinson and after the advances of Henry Aaron, Frank Robinson, Maury Wills, Larry Doby, Cito Gaston, and Bill White, I can still look around the league and see the remnants of the old double standard.

47. Monte Irvin.

48. James Gilliam, infielder for the Brooklyn Dodgers. *Wide World Photos.*

49. Roy Campanella tosses aside his mask as he twists after a foul pop off the bat of Hank Bauer of the New York Yankees in the third inning of a 1956 World Series Game. *Wide World Photos.*

50. Power at the plate: Roy Campanella of the Brooklyn Dodgers. *Wide World Photos.*

To Art
Be Happy
Ernie
Banks
8/22/89

51. Ernie Banks, the premier power hitter par excellance among shortstops. He was perhaps the most popular man ever to play for the Chicago Cubs. Banks had a lifetime total of 512 home runs; was voted the National League's Most Valuable Player in 1958 and 1959. He entered the Baseball Hall of Fame in 1977.

52. Don Newcombe of the Brooklyn Dodgers delivers a pitch in the sixth inning of a game with the St. Louis Cardinals at Ebbets Field, September 19, 1956. Don nailed his twenty-fifth victory with a pitching-hitting parlay that beat the Cardinals 17-2. He walloped a pair of home runs and gave up just seven hits before calling it a day after seven innings. *Wide World Photos.*

53. Strikeout milestone. St. Louis Cardinal right-hander Bob Gibson gives it all he's got in nabbing his 3,000 career strikeout in a night game against the Cincinnati Reds, July 18, 1974. Gibson, 38, fanned Cesar Geronimo to reach the mark that has been achieved by only one other pitcher, Walter Johnson. Gibson won the Cy Young Award in 1968 and 1970, and was voted the Most Valuable Player in 1968. *Wide World Photos.*

54. Baseball's best batsman, Rod Carew of the Minnesota Twins heads for first after one of his many bunts during the 1974 season. Carew locked up his third straight Anerican League batting championship, and fourth since 1969, and ranks as one of the game's premium bunters and base stealers. *Wide World Photos.*

55. Cleon Jones of the New York Mets. *Wide World Photos*.

56. Richie Allen. *Wide World Photos*.

57. Catcher Elston Howard, the first black New York Yankee (1955), spent twelve and a half years in New York before being traded to the Boston Red Sox. *New York Yankees*.

58. Shortstop, third baseman John Kennedy, who in 1957 became the first black on the Philadelphia Phillies.

59. Outfielder Carlos Paula of Havana, Cuba. In 1954, he joined the Washington Senators and became the first black on the roster. *National Baseball Library, Cooperstown, N.Y.*

60. Third baseman Ozzie Virgil. The first black on the Detroit Tigers in 1958.

61. On July 21, 1959, second baseman Elijah "Pumpsie" Green became the Boston Red Sox's first black player. His debut conpleted the cycle: all sixteen major league teams now employed blacks. *Boston Red Sox.*

62. Curt Flood, the St. Louis Cardinals' gifted center fielder from 1958 to 1969. He hit over .300 six times and .293 lifetime. Flood had been traded by the Cardinals to the Philadelphia Phillies in late 1969, but he refused to report to Philadelphia even though he was offered a $100,000 contract. Instead he sued to become a free agent, claiming the "Reserve Clause" making him the lifetime "property" of whatever club holds his contract constituted "involuntary servitude" and was therefore unconstitutional. The United States Supreme Court, however, upheld the status quo. *National Baseball Library, Cooperstown, N.Y.*

63. Reggie Jackson, one of the greatest clutch hitters in baseball history, reached the zenith of his major league career on October 18, 1977, when as a New York Yankee in the sixth game of the World Series against the Los Angeles Dodgers he hit three successive home runs.

64. Brock beats ball for record. Lou Brock of the St. Louis Cardinals slides into second base just ahead of the ball to set the major league record of 105 stolen bases in a single season: September 9, 1974. *Wide World Photos.*

65. At one time the greatest defensive shortstops I ever saw where Marty Marion, Mark Belanger, and Roy McMillan. Now I'm convinced Ozzie Smith is the best fielding shortstop in baseball history.

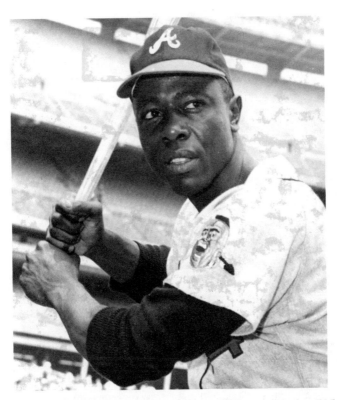

66. Hank Aaron. On April 8, 1974 in Atlanta, he hit home run number 715 to break Babe Ruth's record of 714.

67. Frank Robinson, Most Valuable Player in the National League in 1961 and in the American League in 1966. In October of 1974 he became the first black to be hired as a major league manager and in June of 1977 the first to be fired. He was elected to the Baseball Hall of Fame in 1982.

68. Dave Winfield. The New York Yankees in December 1980 shocked major league baseball by signing free agent Winfield to a ten-year contract for between $13 and $25 million. Winfield had eight great seasons with the San Diego Padres and went on to have superb years with the Yankees. A fantastic outfielder, Winfield will go down in history as one of the New York Yankees' greatest defensive outfielders. He has a "soft" hand and a powerful, accurate throwing arm. His leaping catches, with all of his 6-foot-6 frame fully extended, glove high, are already legendary. *New York Yankees.*

69. Felix Millan. *Wide World Photos.*

70. Roberto Clemente played the outfield for the Pittsburgh Pirates from 1955 to 1972, hitting .317 and smacking 240 home runs. He died in a plane crash in 1972 while taking supplies for the relief of Nicaraguan earthquake victims. The five-year waiting period for election to the Hall of Fame was waived and he was elected the following year.

71. Darryl Strawberry. He endured eight difficult years with the New York Mets. The rightfielder grew up in Los Angeles and was the Mets first-round draft pick in 1980 shortly after graduating from Crenshaw High School. Strawberry became a full-time major leaguer in the 1983 season and won National League Rookie of the Year honors. When he left the Mets, he did so as their all-time leading home run hitter (.252). He joined the Los Angeles Dodgers the winter of 1990, with a $20.25 million contract for five years. *Louis Requena.*

72. Orlando Cepeda. *Wide World Photos.*

73. Luis Aparicio. *Wide World Photos.*

THEIR TONGUE
WILL TELL

The late Roberto Clemente once said, "When the sportswriters write about a black or Hispanic player, it's always something controversial. When they write about white players, it's usually nice—human interest stuff."

ROBERTO CLEMENTE

"It is harder for a Puerto Rican or a Latin ballplayer. People do not want to give them work off the field. So no one knows them. I would make a lot more money in baseball if I were a white American."

Roberto Clemente

"Baseball survives because guys like Clemente still play it."

Jimmy Cannon

For more than fifty years Latin Americans have played major league baseball, most of them coming from Cuba, but more recently from Puerto Rico. Adolpho Luque, who for some twenty years hurled for Boston, Cincinnati, Brooklyn, and New York in the National League, and "Good Field No Hit" Mike

Gonzales, Havana-born backstop for Boston, Cincinnati, St. Louis, and New York, were the only two Latins prior to 1947 who attained any success in the big leagues.

When Jackie Robinson joined the Brooklyn Dodgers in 1947, major league clubs really started digging for Spanish-speaking ballplayers from Puerto Rico, the Virgin Islands, Mexico, Venezuela, Cuba, and just about every single Latin isle. The year-round opportunity to play baseball seemed to bring the Latin players to maturity much sooner. From Havana in 1949 came the colorful Orestes Minoso, who had fifteen fine years in the majors with Cleveland, Chicago, and Washington in the American League and St. Louis in the National League.

In 1955 the late Roberto Clemente from Puerto Rico joined the Pittsburgh Pirates. Over the years, Clemente was modern baseball's match for Ty Cobb and Honus Wagner. His hitting, running, and throwing were superlative. Clemente would often comment that he knew of no one in the game who could hit, run, throw, and play the outfield better than he could. Had Clemente played in New York, the communication capitol of the world, his name would have long since been echoed from coast to coast.

Despite his constant complaining of aches and pains, there was no one in the majors who played as hard as Clemente did, and pain and discomfort did not always keep him from playing. In 1972 Clemente celebrated his 3,000th hit. He led the National League in batting four times. His arm was deadly, throwing out many a runner and discouraging many from trying for that extra base. His performance for the Pirates in the 1971 World Series against the Baltimore Orioles was one of baseball's greatest single performances by any player in the fall classic. He won the Series almost all by himself with a .414 batting average and at least one hit per contest. He hit two homers, barely missed another, and made two impossible catches in the outfield.

In December 1972 Roberto Clemente died in a plane crash while carrying relief supplies to earthquake victims in Nicaragua. In 1973 sportswriters voted almost unanimously to waive the usual five-year waiting period and admitted Roberto Clemente to the Hall of Fame.

FELIX MILLAN

FELIX MILLAN: When I started playing with Daytona Beach in the Florida State League in 1964, one of the biggest problems for me and other Latin American ballplayers is the fact that when we come to the States we don't know how to speak English good enough to get an understanding with the other American ballplayers. When I came to play at Daytona Beach I had quite a few problems because I couldn't speak good English. I just couldn't make myself understandable. When I wanted to eat when the other players were eating, they wouldn't let me go to the restaurant. Also, sometimes I had to wait in the bus until they brought something for me, because I was black and was not allowed in the restaurant.

It was a little difficult for me at the time, but I'm sure the guys before me had a harder time than I had that year of 1964. Every time we went on a road trip, me and the other Latin American ballplayers had to stick together because we didn't speak good English, and the other problem, like I said before, was eating in the same restaurant with the white guys.

After I left Daytona in 1964, I went to Yakima in the Northwestern League, and that was a little different because it was the Northwest and everybody liked everybody there—the racism wasn't like in Florida. The guys tried to teach me English there, and the managers were nice to me. Then when I went to Austin, Texas, the trouble started again.

Me and another black player, Glen Clark, were driving from Austin, Texas, to West Palm Beach, and we couldn't eat in the restaurants along the way. We had to buy sodas and cake in strange back places.

Right now I think Latin American players should be top executives or managers: guys like Vic Power, Felipe Alou, Ossie Virgil, Jose Pagan, and Luis Aparicio. The Latin American problems in the major leagues are not exactly similar to the black players' problems. To tell you the truth, I think it's worse, because if you don't come from this country, it's tough. The black athletes get together when they want to talk about something. But the Spanish guys are afraid to get together because then we don't speak English and that means it would take us longer to communicate with others. I think what the Latin ballplayers need is bilingual spokesmen representing their concerns to owners and league executives.

SANDY ALOMAR

Sandy Alomar is founder of his own baseball dynasty. His son Sandy Jr. plays catcher for the Cleveland Indians and his other son Roberto is second baseman for the Toronto Blue Jays.

SANDY ALOMAR: One of the main problems of the Latin ballplayers is the language barrier and adjusting to the weather and adjusting to the people. We have different ways of being, different manners. Over here we have to get used to the food and traveling and the cold weather. The biggest problem for the Latin player, however, is the language barrier. If we don't learn English we have a hell of a lot of problems. Most of the Puerto Ricans like myself do have the advantage over the other Spanish players because when we go to school we do have to take English—plus you have a lot of Puerto Ricans here and in Puerto Rico who speak English.

In 1960 when I came up, I was very lucky because I had always been interested in English and always worked with a lot of American guys to learn more English every day. In other words, I mixed. The black and Spanish players have to be a little "extra" than the white players to get the job. Ability-wise we do have to be better, there's no doubt about that.

DAVE CONCEPCION

Dave Concepción rates as an oddity among major league players. While most players of All-Star caliber are paid big bonuses when they sign pro contracts, Concepción said, "Not me. I got no bonus when I signed with the Reds. It cost me $44. When Fred Calvino, the Reds' scout, signed me, he told me no club gives bonuses to Latin players." Asked about the $44, Concepción said, "Calvino gave me a glove and a pair of shoes when I signed the contract. I paid $22 for the glove and $22 dollars for the shoes."

DAVE CONCEPCIÓN: Black and Latin ballplayers have about the same problems with one exception: the language barrier. When I started with Tampa in 1968 I couldn't eat in a lot of places like the white players, but now it's different. I had a lot of trouble with my language because I don't speak good English at all. A lot of managers don't want to keep a lot of the Latin ballplayers in the big leagues simply because they don't understand us. And we don't understand the manager. Sometimes they keep Latin players in the minor leagues longer so they can learn English. I know this as a fact.

Sometimes a manager says something to a Latin player he doesn't understand and it might lead to a fight. At Tampa in 1968 it wasn't that bad, because Tampa is basically a Spanish city and they get a lot of Latin people there. My first year there, because I didn't understand English, I practically had to eat chicken for about six months—that's all I could say. On the Tampa team my first year they had no Spanish players. I roomed with a couple of black brothers; they couldn't understand what I was talking about. The guys would say to me, "Dave, the bus leaves in five minutes," and I missed it all the time because I didn't know what the hell they were talking about.

Right now everything is different; things are strictly business. The Latin players are colorful and bring people to the ballpark. They need us now. We have bad tempers, I will admit that, but we are learning to control ourselves. The real problem with the Latin player is the lack of communication because of the language problem.

EPILOGUE

"It was more than a game, it was life."

It's the 1985 major league baseball season and I'm up in the press box with Bill White, then doing play-by-play for the New York Yankees and now president of the National League. White looks over to me and says, "Hey, Art, we have a lot of black players on the field, but up here in the press box in the print and electronic, you and I are the only blacks." I think it's unbelievable.

St. Nicholas Avenue, stickball games, fantasizing; frustrations, futility; Joe Louis, the guys on the block. All contributing to my dreams. Summer of 1938 . . . getting autographs from the left-field bleachers at the Polo Grounds . . . John Leonard "Pepper" Martin of the St. Louis Cardinals pushing my scorecard aside and saying, "Get out of my way, you little black bastard. Why don't you go and see the niggers play baseball."

In reminiscing about the Jackie Robinson, Roy Campanella, and Don Newcombe years on the Dodgers, St. Louis Cardinals' star Stan Musial once said that had the Cards been as aggressive in seeking out black baseball talent as were the Dodgers, they would have been the dominant team in the National League. He said that he realized that because the Cardinals hadn't opened their clubhouse doors to black players, the team suffered. The Dodgers dominated the National League in the 1950s. They sat right at the top year after year. It was a position the Cards could have occupied, Musial once said, had they only recruited black talent.

Yes, they let Jackie Robinson into the modern major leagues, the first black player to break the barrier. Maury Wills broke Ty Cobb's single-season stolen-base record; this record more recently was broken by another black man, Rickey Henderson. Hank Aaron shattering the cherished Babe Ruth's lifetime home-run mark; the Cleveland Indians' appointment of Frank Robinson as the first black manager in the major leagues. Blacks now in the Hall of Fame!

I always wanted to tell this story. I've attempted to put it down in the preceding pages: a black kid growing up in the white world, listening to white radio, seeing white movies, reading white newspapers, watching white sports. Suffering the humiliation of hearing my first grade teacher, Mrs. Harrington, reading Little Black Sambo aloud to my predominately white class while I wanted to hide under the desk. Yet, despite all these barriers, like Dr. Martin Luther King, Jr., I too had a dream. People laughed at me, but I persevered.

And so, after all, did the heroic men whose stories are recorded in this book. Joe Black was one of the younger generation of ballplayers who attended the 1991 reunion of the last remaining survivers of the old Negro leagues at Cooperstown. Black had been a pitcher for the Dodgers and although he personally did not experience the institutionalized segregation that blighted the sport, he nonetheless remembers it well. And he remembers what made the men who endured—like Josh Gibson, and Satchel Paige, and Buck Leonard—real legends and true heroes.

"All they wanted was to play on that field and play competitively," he said. "It was more than a game, it was life."

Appendix

FIRST BLACKS FOR EACH TEAM IN THE MAJOR LEAGUES

AMERICAN LEAGUE

Cleveland Indians	Larry Doby	1947
St. Louis Browns	Henry Thompson	1947
	Willard Brown	
Chicago White Sox	Sam Hairston	1951
Philadelphia Athletes	Bob Trice	1953
Washington Senators	Carlos Paula	1954
New York Yankees	Elston Howard	1955
Detroit Tigers	Ozzie Virgil	1958
Boston Red Sox	Pumpsie Green	1959

NATIONAL LEAGUE

Brooklyn Dodgers	Jackie Robinson	1947
	Dan Bankhead	
New York Giants	Hank Thompson	1949
	Monte Irvin	
Boston Braves	Sam Jethroe	1950
Chicago Cubs	Gene Baker	1953
	Ernie Banks	
Pittsburgh Pirates	Curt Roberts	1954
St. Louis Cardinals	Tom Alston	1954
Cincinnati Reds	Nino Escalera	1954
Philadelphia Phillies	John Kennedy	1957

BLACKS NAMED AS MOST VALUABLE PLAYERS

AMERICAN LEAGUE

1963	Elston Howard	New York	(C)
1966	Frank Robinson	Baltimore	(OF)
1971	Vida Blue	Oakland	(P)
1972	Richie Allen	Chicago	(1B)
1973	Reggie Jackson	Oakland	(OF)
1977	Rod Carew	Minnesota	(1B)
1978	Jim Rice	Boston	(OF)
1979	Don Baylor	California	(OF)
1987	George Bell	Toronto	(OF)
1990	Rickey Henderson	Oakland	(OF)

NATIONAL LEAGUE

1949	Jackie Robinson	Brooklyn	(2B)
1951	Roy Campanella	Brooklyn	(C)

1953	Roy Campanella	Brooklyn	(C)
1954	Willie Mays	New York	(OF)
1955	Roy Campanella	Brooklyn	(C)
1956	Don Newcombe	Brooklyn	(P)
1957	Hank Aaron	Milwaukee	(OF)
1958	Ernie Banks	Chicago	(SS)
1959	Ernie Banks	Chicago	(SS)
1961	Frank Robinson	Cincinnati	(OF)
1965	Willie Mays	San Francisco	(OF)
1966	Roberto Clemente	Pittsburgh	(OF)
1967	Orlando Cepeda	St. Louis	(1B)
1968	Bob Gibson	St. Louis	(P)
1969	Willie McCovey	San Francisco	(1B)
1976	Joe Morgan	Cincinnati	(2B)
1977	George Foster	Cincinnati	(OF)
1978	Dave Parker	Pittsburgh	(OF)
1979	Willie Stargell	Pittsburgh	(1B)
	Keith Hernandez	St. Louis	(1B)
1985	Willie McGee	St. Louis	(OF)
1987	Andre Dawson	Chicago	(OF)
1989	Kevin Mitchell	San Francisco	(OF)
1990	Barry Bonds	Pittsburgh	(OF)

BLACKS NAMED AS
ROOKIE OF THE YEAR

AMERICAN LEAGUE

1966	Tommie Agee	Chicago	(OF)
1971	Chris Chambliss	Cleveland	(1B)
1973	Al Bumbry	Baltimore	(OF)
1977	Eddie Murray	Baltimore	(DH)
1978	Lou Whitaker	Detroit	(2B)
1979	Alfredo Griffin	Toronto	(SS)
1984	Alvin Davis	Seattle	(1B)
1985	Ozzie Guillen	Chicago	(SS)

NATIONAL LEAGUE

1947	Jackie Robinson	Brooklyn	(1B)
1949	Don Newcombe	Brooklyn	(P)
1950	Sam Jethroe	Boston	(OF)
1951	Willie Mays	New York	(OF)
1952	Joe Black	Brooklyn	(P)
1953	Jim Gilliam	Brooklyn	(2B)
1956	Frank Robinson	Cincinnati	(OF)
1958	Orlando Cepeda	San Francisco	(1B)
1959	Willie McCovey	San Francisco	(1B)
1961	Billy Williams	Chicago	(OF)
1964	Dick Allen	Philadelphia	(3B)
1971	Earl Williams	Atlanta	(C)
1973	Gary Matthews	San Francisco	(OF)
1974	Bake McBride	St. Louis	(OF)
1977	Andre Dawson	St. Louis	(OF)
1983	Darryl Strawberry	New York	(OF)
1984	Dwight Gooden	New York	(P)

1985	Vince Coleman	St. Louis	(OF)
1989	Jerome Walton	Chicago	(OF)
1990	Dave Justice	St. Louis	(OF)

BLACKS NAMED AS
BATTING CHAMPIONS

AMERICAN LEAGUE

1964	Tony Oliva	Minnesota	.323
1965	Tony Oliva	Minnesota	.321
1969	Rod Carew	Minnesota	.332
1970	Alex Johnson	California	.329
1971	Tony Oliva	Minnesota	.337
1972	Rod Carew	Minnesota	.318
1973	Rod Carew	Minnesota	.350
1974	Rod Carew	Minnesota	.364
1975	Rod Carew	Minnesota	.359
1977	Rod Carew	Minnesota	.388
1978	Rod Carew	Minnesota	.333
1982	Willie Wilson	Kansas City	.332
1989	Kirby Pucket	Minnesota	.339
1991	Julio Franco	Texas	.341

NATIONAL LEAGUE

1949	Jackie Robinson	Brooklyn	.342
1954	Willie Mays	New York	.345
1956	Hank Aaron	Milwaukee	.328
1959	Hank Aaron	Milwaukee	.355
1961	Roberto Clemente	Pittsburgh	.351
1962	Tommy Davis	Los Angeles	.346
1963	Tommy Davis	Los Angeles	.326
1964	Roberto Clemente	Pittsburgh	.339
1965	Roberto Clemente	Pittsburgh	.329
1966	Matty Alou	Pittsburgh	.342
1967	Roberto Clemente	Pittsburgh	.357
1970	Rico Carty	Atlanta	.366
1972	Billy Williams	Chicago	.333
1974	Ralph Garr	Atlanta	.353
1975	Bill Madlock	Chicago	.354
1976	Bill Madlock	Chicago	.339
1977	Dave Parker	Pittsburgh	.338
1978	Dave Parker	Pittsburgh	.334
1981	Bill Madlock	Pittsburgh	.341
1982	Al Oliver	Montreal	.331
1983	Bill Madlock	Pittsburgh	.323
1984	Tony Gwynn	San Diego	.351
1985	Willie McGee	St. Louis	.353
1986	Tim Raines	Montreal	.334
1987	Tony Gwynn	San Diego	.370
1988	Tony Gwynn	San Diego	.313
1989	Tony Gwynn	San Diego	.336
1990	Willie McGee	St. Louis	.335
1991	Terry Pendleton	Atlanta	.319

74. Record breaker. Henry Aaron, at bat in the fourth inning of the Atlanta
Braves–Los Angeles Dodgers game at Atlanta Stadium, April 8, 1974, made sports
history with this swing. It was his 715th major-league home run. *Wide World
Photos.*

Index